ACCELERATE YOUR SUCCESS

LET'S GO!

A COACHING GUIDE TO DISCOVERING WHAT'S NEXT AND PURSUING IT

MAZIE MINEHART COLEN, M.S.

EXECUTIVE COACH

Author's note: The identifiers and details of the coaching examples provided in this book have been changed to respect the confidentiality of the coaching relationships.

ISBN: 979-8-218-44935-3

Publisher MMC Executive Coaching & Consulting, LLC

For information regarding special discounts for bulk purchases, please contact
mazie@mmcexeccoach.com

This book is dedicated to you.

Thank you for investing in yourself and your future.
Imagine if we all did!

CONTENTS

Introduction

No matter where you are in your career and life, if you are reading this book, you are ready for change. Whether you have been working in the same industry for 30 years and wondering what's next or whether you are just graduating from college and wanting to make a career plan, we can all benefit from evaluating our path and being more deliberate about planning for what comes next. Picking up this book is your first step to taking action, so "Let's Go!"

Today is a great day to start.

Each day, my morning begins with a walk outside, prompted by my dog, Stella. My sweet 22-pound labradoodle waits patiently at the door until I leash her and shout, "Let's Go!" Rain or shine, I don't overthink it; I lace up my shoes and go. Once outside, the community comes alive around us. People are on the move, heading to work or school. Recently, my neighbor David ran out to join me on my walk with his dog. David is an international pharmaceutical company executive and has shared anecdotes with me for years about challenges with his team or company changes. On this particular morning in early January, David confidentially revealed he was having a midlife crisis and wanted to talk. He shared that he needed to collaborate with someone who understood his internal struggle. As an executive coach for over 30 years, I am often asked, "Do you have a minute to discuss my current challenge?" I am always eager to help those around me. Yet, the struggle is an essential part of finding the path. Each time I am privileged to hear someone's story, I reflect on how this universal tendency to question ourselves is part of our journey.

We all live complex lives with many roles to play. At certain points in our lives, we question. It is productive to consider if we are spending our time on the right things and to check in to see if we are intentionally moving in a direction we desire to reach. We can also seek guidance and discover a better path when we feel lost.

This book is for those questioning and seeking course correction or the best upcoming path. Are you feeling stuck personally? Do you have a conflict at work you are trying to solve? Are you questioning if you are in the right career? I am eager to share some wisdom I have learned from working with my clients over the past 30 years. My coaching process is a cumulative story learned from my client's challenges and triumphs. From years of collaboration, I have captured a process that has been helpful to guide them, and I hope to help you.

Reading this, you are already becoming the person you aspire to be. Taking action gives us a sense of control over our destinies. Rather than simply floating along in life and seeing what comes our way, this book intends to help you consider the answers to the big questions and create a roadmap to achieve what you want. It is an action plan that will take you to your unique destination. Regardless of where you may find yourself, let's go together now; I urge you to claim this moment as an opportunity to improve. You are on the move now; let's accelerate together.

Rather than simply floating along in life and seeing what comes our way, this book intends to help you consider the answers to the big questions and create a roadmap to achieve what you want.

My path to coaching was not a straight line. People often ask, "How did you become an executive coach?" As a college athlete, I always valued my relationships with my coaches before recognizing that this profession could also apply to business and life. Pushing potential to higher performance, building confidence through practice, and visualizing success were early concepts for me. After putting my lacrosse stick down and graduating from Brown University, I joined a start-up that evolved into a consulting company. Working with ambitious and successful role models, I had a front-row seat to learn about leadership. While earning my master's degree, I could test and practice the concepts directly from my studies in organizational development. I have been coaching and training executive leaders in business since 1995.

Throughout my career, I learned that being a great leader starts with self-awareness and is strengthened by a commitment to continuous growth and practice. I realized that the key to facilitating a great conversation is not having the answers but knowing what questions to ask. My role has always been to be a deep listener, to truly internalize what leaders say with what they share, and then to reflect the essence of their goals meaningfully back to them. Think about this: who besides you is an expert on you? I know it is a silly question, but *you* are the best expert on you!

I am merely here as a guide. The process that I share in the pages ahead includes the practices I have used and the information I've gathered from client experiences and experts.

Stella and I will continue our walks every morning, where a casual encounter may lead to an aha moment or a new idea to try. Yet, for those who won't bump into me on the dog walk, this book is for you.

Don't just talk about it, be about it. And if you are gonna be about it, you better be allllll about it.

It's time to put your foot on the accelerator pedal. Let's go!

Starting Together: Defining Our Roles and Setting Ourselves Up for Success

When is the right time to start working on your future?

Right now! Now is a great time to start, so tap into this motivation. When change is calling, you should answer that call. If you wonder what is "next" for you or feel challenged by a complex problem, don't overthink, overanalyze, or get stuck in a pros-and-cons comparison.

We often long to make a change when we face a transition, when we get a new opportunity, or when we start a new year. Sometimes, we set goals when facing a significant life milestone. If you are at a point where you want something different or want to shake things up, having a partner, a sounding board, or a guide is helpful. Everyone can benefit from a relationship with a coach. I'm sharing the actual process I use with clients so you can experience it with me now.

The primary question I ask every client to initiate our first discussion is, "How can I help?" This fundamental question clarifies our roles and my intentions, and, most importantly, it nudges you to identify and articulate what you need or want to happen. The question prompts discussion, collaboration, and exploration. In addition, taking the time to state the primary reason for picking up this book starts our journey together.

A famous quote attributed to Buddha reads, "When the learner is ready, the teacher will appear." Years ago, I took a yoga class, and the instructor began the practice by saying aloud, "I'd like to introduce you to your teacher for today's class." Then he told us to put our hands on our hearts and meet our teacher. He wanted us to listen to ourselves as we are our best teachers.

I found this concept profound and relevant to the art of coaching. We sometimes need to remember to listen to our own voices. Perhaps our lives have grown too noisy to hear ourselves. And even if we are open to listening to ourselves loud and clear, we may feel uncertain about how to accomplish the change.

I am eager to be your guide to help you listen more deeply to your voice. This process taps into your thinking and ideas and prompts you to be in the driver's seat. I am your navigator, and you are at the wheel. Remember, you are the truest expert on you. When you motor through this process with me, you will learn more about yourself, clarify your goals, identify roadblocks, and employ practical strategies to remove them. So, now it is time to engage, take action, make commitments, and enjoy the journey.

Introducing The 4D Process

As with any worthwhile project, there is preparation, decision, effort, and evaluation. This process will ensure we can measure results in areas that may be hard to measure. I call this process the **4D process**. The four phases are Discover, Decide, Deliver, and Debrief.

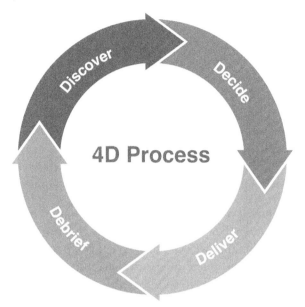

Discover is the essential first step, sometimes the most valuable, as it will reveal a new awareness and a foundation to work from for years ahead. It is imperative to *identify where you are today and what success looks like* for you. While the approach may seem simplistic, the discovery phase is packed with some thought-provoking questions to uncover the big picture. Please take this process one step at a time and be patient. Taking time to discover allows us to methodically and purposefully identify what we want before we take action toward our desired goals.

I like to use a journey analogy for this work. Think of a voyage to a distant land you have always wanted to visit. In the Discover phase, we will be taking the steps to build a solid and seafaring boat to use for this journey. We must take this step. Too often, we hear of strategies or quick fixes, or we take on other people's definitions of success, which leads us to waste time.

Decide is when we identify and commit to specific *goals*. Once we have the seafaring boat, we must pick a destination or goal for our work together. In the Decide phase, we identify our targets and prepare to move toward that target.

Deliver is when we take *action* toward our goal. This phase is the journey itself, when progress happens, and up-leveled behaviors begin to be implemented and demonstrated—the "just do it" phase. In the Deliver phase, we practice new behaviors and ways of thinking and troubleshoot many challenges that might derail us from our path to accomplishment. In this phase, you can learn from my client's experiences and use your tools to form habits that will ensure your success. Often, there are surprises or challenges in our journey toward accomplishment. I have included many suggestions for troubleshooting these unexpected challenges.

Debrief is when we deconstruct what happened, look back, and evaluate what to do differently next time. In the Debrief phase, we reflect and *learn from our own* experiences. Think of this as your journey back from a destination, when you take time to reflect and review so your next trip can be even better. We will also cover common challenges, such as dealing with conflict, navigating transitions, and handling a crisis. When we debrief, we often identify our next set of targets and goals. The Debrief phase of the process feeds back to Discovery.

Albert Einstein theorized that there is a fourth dimension in time and space beyond what we can see. The 4D process enables us to get to that dimension that we can't quite see just yet, but we will uncover; it is the potential for what can be. Doing this work will help you feel differently, have a sense of accomplishment, and be in a better place. It's time to engage in this 4D process, level up, and make things happen.

Knowing Your Starting Point

By this point, you can probably tell I don't like to waste any time. I am direct and action-oriented, pushing my clients toward real change. Once you start, the momentum will grow, so let's get this process in motion! Buckle up, get out of your comfort zone, grab a pen or a pencil, and Let's Go!

Why did you pick up this book?

- Is there a problem you are trying to solve in your business?

- Are you trying to improve your personal effectiveness?

- Do you have an opportunity to achieve something grand and need support?

- Are you avoiding a challenge?

- Are you wondering "what's next" for your work or life?

Now, I need you to take action and use pen and paper. Don't hesitate. Step into action so you can visibly see yourself already making progress. We will get to the big, bigger, biggest picture later—but for now, capture your idea here. What comes to mind first? Do not overthink!

Writing this thought down is starting the work. Simply take a minute to jot down what you decide to work on *right now*.

What I am going to change in my life: _____

_____

Each client I work with has a primary need, a current challenge, or an opportunity. I call this the **presenting problem**. You just wrote down the original reason you picked up this book. However, to make sense of that presenting problem, we need to dig deeper and start at the foundation so that this all makes sense—even to you. I want to meet you where you are and help you uncover *why* this is your current focus.

Defining Your *Why*

Defining *why* you want to change will ignite the energy and actions for what comes next.

The reason *why* is very personal—one only you can answer. Most people like to skip this essential first step as they make assumptions regarding why they need to make a change. Commonly, I find people are interested in jumping right to the *how* before they answer the *why*. How do I change? How do I start? Yet, please consider that the purpose behind our actions is often the most important thing. Once we know our *why*, we can tackle any *what* or *how*; I can help you answer the *how* by walking you through the process and providing you with all the steps along the way; leave the *how* to me.

Let's explore *why* you want to make this change. Is it an opportunity on the horizon—a new job or role? Do you want to change some aspect of your life, such as a habit or behavior? *Why* are you eager to make this change in your life? Is the change worthy of your attention and your commitment? What needs to change or fall away for there to be a shift in your focused attention? Here are some helpful questions to help clarify your *why*.

- Why make this change? _____

- What results would you get if you made this change? _____

_____

- What would happen if you did not make this change? _____

  _____

- What will this change help you avoid or gain? _____

  _____

- Why now? Why is this the right time to make this change? _____

  _____

You are the leader of your own life; you are in charge. Take another minute with these questions to make sure you answer them completely.

What if I don't full in? change? outside influences

Simon Sinek shared the concept of starting with *why* in his book *Start with Why: How Great Leaders Inspire Everyone to Take Action.* Sinek's book seems written for a business audience, yet the message resonates more universally. This simple yet powerful message is relevant for everyone making a change.

Throughout this book, I will reference leadership books I share with my clients. If you want to stick with the process and go quickly, you can always return to these recommendations later. Sometimes it's good to tap into your energy to get started quickly.

Finding the Energy to Start

The difference between doing nothing and doing something is a big amount of energy. When we make a decision—to start a diet, to clean out the garage, to write a book—breaking the inertia takes the most energy. Isaac Newton states in the first law of motion, "An object at rest stays at rest, and an object in motion stays in motion." This is also known as the law of inertia. Forward motion creates momentum. We will amplify our energy for change, leading to greater motivation and capacity for approaching the path ahead. Once we define our *why*, then we can commit to the process. Committing to the process and doing the work to drive the outcomes you want is essential. The benefits of the process are as important as the destination. There are no quick fixes or shortcuts.

When I was 35, I hired a nutrition coach. I was motivated and eager to make changes. The experience was informative and eventually re-vamped my entire relationship with food. I vividly remember my first meeting with my coach. I requested that she take me through her six-month program in six weeks. I told her I was an overachiever and already had a lot of prior knowledge about nutrition. I suggested in our first meeting that I wanted a meal plan to know what to eat, and I would comply with whatever she suggested. It was summertime, and I was motivated to get on a plan and get results for my beach vacation.

When I engaged in the process, even in our first meeting, there was much more information than I expected, and the process had a big learning curve. Yet, I just wanted a know-what-to-eat shortcut. My coach challenged my long-held beliefs about food until that point. I realized these beliefs, which I considered accurate and truthful facts, were now proven scientifically to be out of date. Now, I had some choices to make. I needed to set up new habits, such as ways of cooking and places I shopped. I'd have to step outside the familiar for new, healthy food. A worthwhile journey often begins with discomfort.

I was excited yet apprehensive about starting the work. I thought I could learn about the program and then take some time to decide if it was a good fit. I felt ready to act when she presented me with evidence that some of the things in my refrigerator were harmful. Was I educated enough to know what good replacement options there would be? No. I decided to sign up and commit to the change that day anyway. The more I knew, the more I didn't know. I knew I had a refrigerator full of "unhealthy" food. How confident was I in preparing the next meal for myself or my kids? I took the motivation and energy from not knowing and decided to use the discord to jump in and try this new relationship with food. I found many great outcomes aligned with better health from doing the work and trusting the process.

Being ready and open to learning is the key to success in nourishing ourselves and evolving on our life's journey. We will take inventory and use our energy to move ahead to something better.

Getting Ready Physically and Mentally

It's time to check in with yourself and take your vital signs. Are you engaged right now? Are you ready for what is next, or do you need a pep talk? Take a quick assessment of your energy. We need your physiology to be ready for what is next. You will need to stoke your motivation in ways that are right for you right now to be in the mental framework or mental state where you can envision outcomes that are possible and within reach. It's time to ensure your internal dialogue with yourself aligns with the most successful outcome you can imagine.

Both mind and body are powerful in creating a state of energy, motivation, and the framework for achievement. Advances in the scientific study of human beings point out that our minds can affect our physical health and vice versa. Let's use our awareness of the mind-body connection to our advantage, giving us a higher probability of achieving our goals.

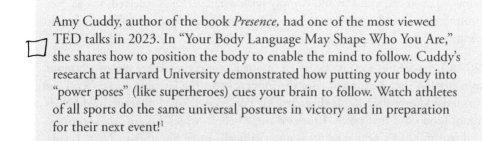

Amy Cuddy, author of the book *Presence,* had one of the most viewed TED talks in 2023. In "Your Body Language May Shape Who You Are," she shares how to position the body to enable the mind to follow. Cuddy's research at Harvard University demonstrated how putting your body into "power poses" (like superheroes) cues your brain to follow. Watch athletes of all sports do the same universal postures in victory and in preparation for their next event![1]

Do not underestimate the power of taking a brisk walk throughout the day to clear your head and raise your energy. Being outside and breathing in the fresh air allows us to stimulate our senses. This practice is a quick and direct way to align our body and mind for change. Our senses are always hard at work, giving our brain data about our environments. So, let's never discount the powerful benefits of deep breaths, an increased heart rate with a brisk walk, peaceful sounds, and all the other sensory elements that help us prepare for our work together. Ramp up inwardly with awareness before you attempt to ramp up externally for change.

Stocking Your Toolbox

Being physically and mentally ready for change is essential, and we also need tools to make tangible progress toward our goals. Using proven tools will strengthen our commitment to our intended actions. They can help keep us motivated and energized to continue our efforts. For example, when we write things down or tell others about a goal, we are more likely to accomplish it.

Here are four tools that have been proven to help my clients make lasting changes. Consider these as part of your toolbox starting now.

 JOT IT   **REFLECT**

 JOURNAL IT   **BUDDY UP**

JOT IT Being Accountable to Yourself

We need to get real for a quick minute.

Are you writing down the answers to these questions in this book, or are you thinking of the answers and just reading on from there?

If you leave the answers floating in the universe, I encourage you to put pen (or pencil) to paper. I get it if you prefer to write things in a journal or notebook instead of this book. If that's the case, find that journal now—seriously. If we do this work together, let's do it. Jot things down and make notes. Underline and highlight. Capture some inspiring affirmations in the margins—whatever helps you commit and personalize doing the actual work. There is space for you to write in this book, with tools to support the integration of your efforts.

Did you know that writing things down makes you more likely to accomplish them? If you simply skip this step and say I am just thinking of my answers, that does not do the trick! I encourage you to grab your favorite pen (or pencil) and write down your most important ideas.

When working with a client, I take a crazy amount of notes. I like to write everything down and then review the notes and consider what resonates most. When I see a client taking notes, that is when I know that something we discussed really hits home. When words are written down, they lead to action. Often, I compare notes with clients. I urge them to write things down with me and with their own teams at work.

Make time to write things down through this process as well. It will pay off.

- We can hold ourselves accountable when we write things down and have a record.

- Writing things down lets our brain see things more visually and is a simple reminder to accomplish things.

CLIENT PEEK

Throughout this book, I share insights from decades of client conversations —all anonymously, of course, in "Client Peek" boxes—so that you have practical, real-life examples to consider while on this journey.

I have some clients who do not write things down in our meetings. Taking notes is a powerful tool, and it makes an impression. One client, who was focused on establishing himself in his new role as CFO, defended his ability to listen and retain information without taking notes in meetings. Many people have this ability, yet it is not always about retaining the information; it is also about the impressions we make. I helped this client recognize that his first impression was very casual, and perhaps he was being perceived as being overconfident and having a bit of an ego. He was confident, a great listener, and perceptive, yet depending on the audience, this might not come across in a conversation. I suggested he take a notebook to his next meeting with his CEO. This client reported that his boss noticed when he pulled out his notebook and took notes in the meeting. This was a visual demonstration that he was listening to his boss. It was also a nonverbal way to communicate that the ideas shared hold power, and there might be action or follow-up based on what is written in the notebook. Consider taking a notebook into your next meeting if this is not something you already do and see if there is an impact.

Some people are not as visual as others and may not feel the need to write things down. My husband often goes to the market without any list; he hears me shout out the items we need and has a knack for remembering them. However, no matter how sharp or accurate your memory is for keeping lists, leaving a paper trail is great for future reference. For our work together, please consider writing things down!

 JOURNAL IT Listening to Your Inner Voice

Journaling is different for many of us. I am not talking about keeping a diary under your pillow to share your innermost secrets. I am simply talking about a place to capture your thoughts.

Have you known process-oriented people who seem to think as they speak and figure things out after sharing out loud? Journaling helps us capture the inner dialogue in the same way. In this forum, you get to converse with yourself and, therefore, have a chance to listen to yourself without judgment. Since you and I can't sit face-to-face for a weekly check-in, I must rely on you to leverage this powerful tool. Spaces throughout this book will help you capture your thoughts, yet they are different from a journal.

A journal helps to create that relationship with your inner voice. Inner thoughts are often the most potent enablers and powerful barriers we face. So, get to know your voice by writing down your internal thought patterns throughout this process. A journal is a perfect place to have that conversation.

There is no need to overthink what you *should* write down; just write what your inner voice is saying. I need you to be patient with this process so we can deeply understand and uncover the truth. The depth of your listening will be up to you. Get quiet. Be patient and wait for the inner voice to communicate clearly. If you search for the truth, for what you are saying, you'll hear yourself—simply if you listen.

 REFLECT Assessing Yourself Authentically

When I ask clients what part of our work has brought them the most value, many tell me that they most appreciate that I am holding up a mirror for them to evaluate themselves accurately and honestly. So, now I ask you to look into the metaphorical mirror or walk right into your bathroom and look in a real-life mirror at any point. Use this tool; it brings results.

Have you ever had the experience where you needed to give a presentation, prepare it, and read it to yourself in the mirror? The mirror does not lie. While this may seem juvenile or theatrical, practicing in the mirror is an excellent tool. When you look at your reflection, you are practicing in real time. You are not just thinking about what you will do but practicing. Our brains need the experience of doing; you can also give yourself real-time feedback and try again.

When I talk about looking in the mirror with my clients, I mean as a metaphor *and* as a tool to employ. If we take that good, honest look at ourselves, we can get information about what is going well and what needs to change.

 BUDDY UP Finding an Accountability Buddy

We are much more successful when we have a trusted person to hold us accountable. If you commit to a workout at the gym and tell your friend that you will be there, you will likely go. If you don't go, you are not just letting yourself down but also letting down your gym partner. If you are trying to change your eating habits and have someone you live with committed to similar health goals, you can keep each other accountable. This works with professional goals as well.

I will be your buddy, and it will be so beneficial if you also pick someone you know personally in your real life to join you on this journey.

Consider who might be able to be your accountability partner in this process. Is there someone at work or in your personal life who would be eager to serve as a sounding board for you or would benefit from experiencing this process with you? Is there a person you could call as you reach milestones who would be thrilled to help you celebrate personal wins? Get them directly involved soon to experience this process together. See your phone? Text or call a buddy. There's no time like right now!

You have your tools. I will prompt you to use each: pen or pencil, the journal, the mirror, and your buddy. You have the power to engage right now in this journey for change!

 Setting Ourselves Up for Success: Key Takeaways

- You are in the driver's seat, and this is your unique journey, so participate!

- The 4D process includes Discover, Decide, Deliver, and Debrief. It builds upon itself and is cyclical.

- Defining your *why* is the essential first step.

- The process is the journey. There are no quick fixes, and the process yields results all along the way. Tap into your energy now!

- Your toolbox includes taking a note, creating a dialogue with yourself by journaling, looking at yourself in the mirror, and finding an accountability buddy.

PHASE 1: DISCOVER

Establishing the Foundation for What Is Next

Let's jump into phase 1, Discover. We have identified your presenting problem, so now it is time to dig in and immerse yourself in the first phase of this process.

This section has many questions for you to answer. These are significant questions and take time to marinate. Therefore, write down the answers as you go. The work builds upon itself, so make sure not to skip any questions that arise. Use the four tools in your toolbox to capture your thinking.

Some of the questions that I ask you to answer are deep and complex. I humbly request that you ponder each question and answer for today. You might want to return to these questions in the future, as some of your answers may change over time. Self-reflection can be tricky. With pure intentions and beneficial past outcomes, I ask you to consider doing the hard labor this section requires. We must lay a solid foundation here to build the rest of the change you want to see. These days, with wild weather and unexpected climate shifts, we can value a solid foundation. Should it arise, resist the temptation to cheat yourself out of the solid ground you may discover. Proceed and take this precious time to explore your unique answers.

We are simply building the foundation, which will bring clarity for the next steps.

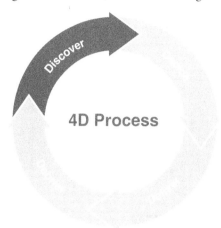

We will tackle discovery in **two parts**: first, looking at yourself as you are now and, then, looking at your aspirations and who you want to become.

- **First, all about you—look at you now.** We look at who we are today and take inventory. We need this exact starting point; it is essential. I want "you" to get to know "you," which will unfold throughout this process.

- **Second, who you want to be—what success looks like to *you*.** Here, we will think about and uncover who you would like to become.

It seems simple, right? Affecting change can also be elusive, slow, measured, or fast. However, the answers to our questions seldom sit at the surface.

Revisiting Your Presenting Problem

We need to determine if the problem we are trying to solve is the root of the problem, not just a symptom of something larger. When working with my clients, I often remark that I'm not available to help straighten deck chairs on the *Titanic*. Looking for quick fixes on the surface, like straightening chairs or organizing our desks or trying new productivity habits without determining what we seek, will not lead to meaningful change or purposeful work. The questions that we cover in the Discover phase will ensure that we are getting to the root causes and the essential values and build the foundation for goals that we want to pursue to achieve our desired outcomes. There is no quick answer for my neighbor, David, about a midlife crisis. Buying a new car will not address what is nagging underneath these uncomfortable feelings. If we do the work outlined in Discover, we will have the foundation for what comes next.

🔍 CLIENT PEEK

This client example illustrates the value of starting the process and seeing it through, challenging the presenting problem to get it right.

Presenting problem: A client reached out to me with the goal of getting a promotion at work and wanted to talk about how to get his company to support him in going back to school for his master's in business administration (MBA).

His initial *why*: Getting an MBA would make him more credentialed and valuable to his company.

Discover: When we walked through the Discover process together (what we will do in this section), we realized that getting an MBA would not necessarily result in a promotion. A credential is great, yet that was not what was holding this client back in his career. Instead, we uncovered the key barrier to his getting a promotion when we discussed feedback he had received from his manager. Through our discussions, we discovered that this client needed to work on critical relationships and his ability to collaborate more with others. Discovery helps us investigate the whole picture and see what drops out as a place to focus when we reach the next phase, Decide. Then, we can set a goal that addresses the true root cause of the problem and get after solving it.

Decide: We were able to set specific goals related to how this client could strengthen his interpersonal skills and how he could build collaboration into his daily work.

Deliver: Over six months, this client was able to practice new behaviors, use new language, and strengthen his awareness of why focusing on interpersonal skill building and collaboration were key to his performance.

people are afraid of others "watching them grow"

Debrief: Eventually, we could look back at all the habits formed, the new practices, and the new relationships this leader had established. He is now focused on deciding his next goal related to his awareness of the greater organization and how he can be seen as a thought leader among his peers. Even without the MBA credential, the company is positioning this leader for a promotion.

Assessing You Now

The "You Are Here" target is the first thing to locate when looking at a map. We need to know our starting point and how to navigate toward our future. The following questions will help clarify your starting point or current state.

In this first part of discovery, our focus is on raising self-awareness and getting to know yourself. You are the expert on yourself, so take time when answering the following questions.

WHAT MAKES YOU GREAT?

We all have natural gifts. My philosophy for coaching starts with identifying strengths. We need to leverage our strengths and move toward what we are good at or what interests us most. What makes you come alive and light up? Indeed, throughout our school years and work experiences, we have grown accustomed to focusing first on self-improvement opportunities. We seldom focus on what *is* working. Some Human Resource practices, such as performance reviews and feedback tools, provide methods for identifying weaknesses or development opportunities. In my experience, when a manager gives an employee feedback, it is often constructive. Our brain looks for deficits or sees a glass half-empty. We tend to focus our attention on the areas we must improve upon first. While there is a place for that, in a new relationship or conversation, most of us don't want to start thinking about what is wrong or what is a deficit; we would rather start with what is working.

In 2001, Marcus Buckingham came on the scene with a groundbreaking book called *Now Discover Your Strengths*. In it, he provides an assessment so people can name their strengths based on decades of research he performed through the Gallup organization. At the time, this work introduced a massive shift from the prior business literature. Before Buckingham's research, corporations looked at competencies and deficits for leaders to improve. Organizational/development practices focused on what was wrong with the organization instead of what was right. "Appreciative inquiry" was introduced in the late 1990s to consider the radical idea of starting with what works in a strategy session instead of with what is not working.

Starting with Strengths

As we get rolling, let's identify what you are good at and what you do well.

We all want to do things that we are good at, right? Why not? Your words are for your eyes only, go for it. Start strong, list your strengths, and maybe list the skills you have always naturally possessed.

Don't think too profoundly—keep moving along and answering the questions.

JOT IT How would you describe yourself? What adjectives would you use?

_____

_____

Now, go deeper.

What are you good at?

Tom Peter's Brand Yu

1. _____

2. _____

3. _____

4. _____

5. _____

What are you known for?

1. _____

2. _____

3. _____

4. _____

5. _____

Keep going as long as you need. Brainstorm here until you think your list is complete.

Other People's Perspective

Now, consider this from other people's perspectives. Think about your colleagues or your friends' points of view. If I were to visit with your closest colleagues or friends and ask them to describe you, what would they say?

JOT IT How would people describe you?

1. _____

2. _____

3. _____

4. _____

5. _____

Did that list come quickly? Did you have to think about specific people, like "My spouse would describe me as _____," or "My current manager/ boss would describe me as _____"? Thinking back to your last formal performance review or the last time your spouse described you, what characteristics come to the top of the list? We need a detailed and complete picture. Add any additional thoughts to the previous lists before you proceed.

With total transparency, now answer the following question.

JOT IT How would you *like* other people to describe you?

1. _____

2. _____

3. _____

4. _____

5. _____

 REFLECT Now compare the previous two lists. What stands out most? Are the adjectives and character elements different or similar?

Take note of the most significant difference between the previous lists: how people might describe you and how you would *like* them to represent you instead.

If I were to take out a billboard for You, Inc., what would you want it to say? What is your intended outbound message? Do you show the world exactly what you plan to offer? Are there just one or two things you want to improve?

Our opportunity for growth begins here and now. These traits build your "personal" brand and help create the foundation of your professional identity, which we will explore later in this chapter.

WHAT ARE YOUR PREFERENCES?

When considering a career path ahead—either for a change or for a new beginning—it is hard to begin with an exact target. Let's take it one step at a time. Keep it simple when figuring out the best "next" move by starting with what you like and do not like.

Often, it is easier to identify what you do not want to be doing, where you do not want to live, or what type of work you know you'll hate. Let's start this investigation by capturing what you love and hate in the following lines. Consider the answer in your current role, status, or broader life context.

JOT IT What do you like?

- What is your favorite way to spend your time? _____

_____

- What subjects/topics (classes) do you gravitate toward? _____

_____

- What projects most excite you? _____

_____

Let's look at things you know you do *not* like. The converse often reveals more than the original question.

JOT IT What do you despise?

- What (parts of your job) do you dislike or avoid? _____

_____

- What classes/ subjects/activities do you despise? _____

_____

- What is the worst way to spend your time (at work or in your personal life)?

_____

JOURNAL IT If you want to explore any of these questions more fully, pull out your journal.

 Marcus Buckingham published a book in 2022 called *Love + Work*. For the first time, this Gallup-trained researcher suggested taking time to do more things we love and fewer things we "loathe."

This simple but often not easy philosophy has gotten lost along the evolution of work. After all, it is called "work," not "loved activities." If you spend many of your days doing certain tasks and pursuing specific goals, you should make sure to integrate things you love doing into your day job![2]

WHAT CHANGES YOUR ENERGY?

We want to incorporate activities that build our energy. Ideally, we make more energy (not less) through our work. We want to spend time on things that put us into that flow state where we feel we are functioning at our best. If we dread certain activities or despise some of the things we do daily, we can identify those activities and obligations and consider how to manage them differently.

Flow is the goal. This is where we want to live. In positive psychology, a flow state, also known colloquially as being *in the zone*, is a mental state in which a person performing some activity is fully immersed in a feeling of energized focus, full involvement, and enjoyment in the process of the activity.

 A flow state, as Mihaly Csikszentmihalyi and Jeanne Nakamura described, is a state that creates "a feeling where, under the right conditions, you become fully immersed in what you are doing." If you are curious or want more about the flow state, check out Mihaly Csikszentmihalyi's work.[3]

JOT IT Asking the following two questions is helpful when looking for subconscious desires to shine through. Take note of some activities that brought you energy in the past couple of days and things you do that completely zap or drain your passion.

- What did you do today that brought you energy? (I'm in the flow; I don't know where time goes.) _____

- What did you do today that drained your energy? (Time moves so slowly; I think my clock broke.) _____

WHAT IS YOUR STYLE?

Now that we have examined your energy and preferences, the next step is to look at your style. Each of us has certain attributes that affect how we think and behave. We are all born with style preferences based on our personalities, upbringing, and role models. Your personality has most likely affected your life so far. We may already know an essential element of our personality based on whether we thrive being around many people or recharging somewhere we can have solitude. Other clues for our personality exist in how we manage time and make decisions.

You might have taken various assessments at this point in your career or your education. In school, at work, or in many self-improvement books and websites, numerous resources help us understand our style and preferences. When working with other people, the natural question is, what is your personality type?

A quick internet search will produce a lengthy list of tools to assess your personality and behavioral style and predict the jobs you are best suited for. Whether you try the Predictive Index, the Hogan Assessment, the DiSC Profile, or numerous other options, these assessments leave us with reports to interpret and styles to confirm. Many take a Myers-Briggs Personality profile but rarely remember the letters that describe their personality type. While these assessment tools serve great purposes for team building and raising awareness of your impact on others, we will look at the foundational elements and keep things simple, as discussed next.

If you are interested in reading more about the well-known personality assessment tool Myers Briggs, read "A Deeper Look at Myers-Briggs Type Indicator." Most psychologists and researchers agree that personality, by and large, represents a predisposition to our inherited tendencies and a blueprint for our behaviors. Nature and nurture shape us, but our nature often defines us from birth. Our core personality may not vary significantly throughout our lives.

Caliper

Do you still believe in the accuracies of these?

A Deeper Look at the Myers-Briggs Type Indicator

A well-known personality test is the Myers-Briggs Type Indicator (MBTI). This assessment hinges on the work of Carl Jung and the commonly known letter combinations that identify your Myers-Briggs Type. After taking the assessment, your results yield four letters that align with attributes. The attributes measured in this assessment categorize personalities in four terms, commonly referred to as the first letters of the category.

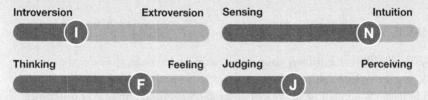

So, your four letters could be a combination like "ISFJ." ISFJ is the most common type. (Intuition is represented by the letter "N," as the "I" was already used for the first measure of Introversion.) So, you might hear people using language like, what's your Myers-Briggs? Your response could be a variety of combined letters. "ENFJ" and "ISTP" are just a few examples.

While there is much controversy regarding the validity of this assessment, many who take the MBTI are surprised, and often their letter/ type is spot-on. If you are interested in satisfying your curiosity, numerous online tools allow you to take the assessment free of charge.

Some psychological journals continue to challenge the validity of Myers-Briggs, yet the attributes it measures have withstood the test of time. This tool is still utilized in many corporations today and is also taught in many colleges and universities. [4]

I have been fortunate to work with many senior leaders who exhibit styles across all personality attributes. While all of the categories are interesting, the introvert-extrovert continuum is one that is frequently discussed in leadership styles. Coaching different energy styles has been part of my practice. Simply, someone who gains energy from being around people is more of an extrovert. Think about yourself. If you have had a full day of work and are committed to an evening networking event tonight, does that energize or drain you? You might be reading this and saying, "How on Earth would it energize me to go to a big social event at the end of a long workday?" Yet, if you're reading this and are an extrovert, you can think of many examples of going to happy hour or work social after a long day and coming home buzzing with energy and not ready for bed. Extroverts get energy from being around people. Spending the entire day working at their "home office" on projects in solitude might be draining for extroverts. They need to get their "charge" with others.

Now, introverts may prefer not to be center stage but rather to recharge in solitude. Before going to a big event, they can spend their day fortifying their energy, possibly alone, so they are ready to face the crowd later. Rather than being tossed into the fray, introverts are usually at their best when they can connect one-on-one. They would prefer not to get on stage where the entire room focuses on them. Conversely, get the extrovert to the stage! When they engage with a full room, the crowd will recharge them like a new battery.

When working with introverted senior leaders, it is helpful to acknowledge the research on the effectiveness of an introverted leader.

If you are looking for more information on introverted leaders, read Susan Cain's work. In her groundbreaking book *Quiet*, Susan Cain helps us understand how introverts can be the most successful in business circles yet often misunderstood. Cain discusses the gifts of the introvert, and it is worth the read if this resonates for you.

Leaders, both introverted and extroverted, can be successful, particularly if they are highly aware of their preferences. Self-awareness is the key.

 CLIENT PEEK

In my experience, I have worked with many extroverted CEOs who have come up the ranks in Sales or Marketing. They frequently lean on their charisma, likeability, and skill in energizing a workforce or inspiring a team. However, I have also worked with numerous CEOs who come up the financial ranks, often moving from CFO to the leadership position of CEO. Commonly, these leaders exhibit classic qualities and attributes most affiliated with introverts. These patient, quiet, thoughtful, and prepared leaders may not be the life of the party in off-site meetings. Yet, they have proven success in forecasting, modeling, and often hitting targets more effectively than some of their more extroverted colleagues.

The crucial element is not the style but rather the self-awareness of your unique style—knowing what helps you build your energy. If you need time to reflect, plan, and work quietly, make time on your calendar. If you need time to collaborate with others, schedule that. Self-awareness is the cornerstone of emotional intelligence, which we will cover in Phase 4 when we discuss emotions in the workplace. Knowing ourselves, our preferences, and our behavioral style makes us even more effective.

 REFLECT Take an honest look at yourself and determine what brings you energy.

Evaluating Your Behavior

While personality types are interesting, my coaching focus has always returned to behavior. We can improve, adjust, or change by working with our behavior. With all the assessments I have used and studied, I've learned two primary factors that shape behavior. The deciding factors are pace (speed) and priority (task or people). Now that you have reflected on what brings you energy let's look at these two factors to see where you may self-assess along a behavioral continuum.

WHAT IS YOUR PACE?

Pace refers to the speed at which you do things, how you process new information, and how you like to navigate relationships. As with any factor, pace can be determined along a continuum. The helpful placement to one side of the median point or the other will yield more information than simply saying you fall right in the center.

Ask yourself what your preferred pace is.

 REFLECT This is a great time to look at your true self. Look in your mirror. Do you like going slow and taking your time? Do you prefer to go fast at any cost, as the fast pace keeps you engaged? Consider the following detailed questions to plot where you are regarding pace.

Where do you see yourself?

Do you like to take your time to get new information? Are you careful? Do you read directions before starting new tasks?

Do you think about previous experiences and mine for clues on how to move forward?

Do you like to go fast and make a move off the cuff before you review?

Do you think faster than others, skip steps, jump ahead, and focus mostly on the future?

Do you speak rapidly in an attempt to communicate the whole story and get impatient when others deliberate?

These are all indicators of your pace.

Do not put too much emphasis on the words used to describe your preferred speed. We could also use words like *careful*, *deliberate*, and *calculated* as synonyms for slow and use words like *speedy*, *quick*, and *swift* for fast.

 JOT IT Put an X on the continuum below to mark your tendencies.

SLOW ——————————————————————————————————————— **FAST**

I bet you know someone whose pace differs vastly from yours. They may be going so slowly that it drives you nuts or speeding ahead so quickly that they tend to miss essential steps. These observations may help you identify why you work so well with some individuals and may feel quite frustrated with others.

Think of someone you know who is slow to act, slow to comment in a meeting, and careful with everything they do. Slow movers want to do things right the first time and get projects correct with efficiency and cautious precision.

Now think of someone you know who is fast-moving, fast-talking, fast-acting—even impulsive at times! They are the first ones to speak up in a meeting. They may think on their feet and always have a comment ready when asked for ideas. They may talk over people in an effort not to forget their thoughts. They may struggle with active listening, and you might notice when they're preparing their response instead of hearing you out first. They think fast and act fast.

Do not make assumptions based on pace!

CLIENT PEEK

I was working with a client from the southern United States who is a disciplined and knowledgeable leader. Speaking with her, at times, felt as slow as molasses. This distinguished leader is a Harvard graduate with a slow, methodical style. And here I was, feeling challenged to slow down and match her pace to work with her. Yet, each time she spoke, I noticed her thoughts were collected, complete, and powerful. Even when the words come out painfully slow (for my brain). She was struggling with colleagues who seemed frustrated with her. I advised her that her style may impact some people in a way that she did not intend. She practiced using cues to share with others. She began meetings by sharing her intention that she was taking her time to get things right for people when she met with them. She was saying more out loud, an easy shift, and she found success. Pace is simply related to style.

There are no good or bad labels here; there are, however, better fits for people whose jobs lean toward the priority that suits them best. Some jobs require us to slow down, be deliberate, and be accurate. Many accountants must compute slowly and accurately. In other professions, speed might be the most essential factor when reacting quickly to a patient's fluctuating situation. The key is to have your style align with your work outcome.

> Who has the fastest speaking pace? People from Minnesota hold the record for speaking faster than any other state in the United States.[5] With its vast geography, the United States is a great place to look at differences in pace. The South is known as "slower" than the Northeast, for example. We make a lot of assumptions based on pace and how people speak and respond to us. Don't let pace prompt inaccurate assumptions.

Different brains work at different paces and speeds. Some people need time to process or digest information. Some people speak more slowly, whereas others do everything quickly. It is important to acknowledge these differences in mental style. The real key is to know your style and own it. If you need time to think, make sure you take that time. And if you are a speedy talker and decision-maker, recognize that this style has benefits, but you may not always be able to bring everyone along.

Often, I will coach my clients to share their intentions related to pace. I suggest they try two strategies: first, to share their intention, and second, to say things out loud. If they intend to match pace with their audience, I prompt them to say, "I'm going to walk through this report with you one step at a time to be sure we catch every detail, as I believe that is your preference." Or, for a faster pace preference, my suggestion would be: "I'm going to breeze through this quickly, so please let me know if I am going too fast or if you want me to slow down." Awareness of our preferences regarding pace helps us bridge with others more effectively to get them comfortable. Always check with your audience for their pace preference first instead of focusing on your own!

WHAT IS YOUR PRIORITY?

Now, let's shift our focus from pace to priorities. I use this term to highlight another continuum, prioritizing people or tasks. Perhaps this is an oversimplification, but our priorities give us important data to work with. A case in point is the revealing "to-do" list. Think about how you like to approach priorities in your day.

- Do you look to accomplish tasks, prioritize reading your email, or prefer doing a project first?

- Do you choose to walk around the office—possibly checking in with people— before you sit down to begin your tasks? Does a better day for you start with a task or with people?

Think about how you prioritize your work: people first or tasks first? Engineers, financial managers, scientists, and many more professions require our task focus. Sales professionals, inspirational speakers, social workers, and other professions where relationships are the cornerstone require a people focus. Some are successful because of their ability to stay focused on the tasks at hand. Some are comfortable working in a closed-door office without much human interaction all day, all week. They are deeply engaged in the task, and nothing and no one else matters. Others have difficulty completing tasks in the office, where there are many opportunities for social interactions, building relationships, and interpersonal connections, and they get "nothing done."

 REFLECT Take a minute to think about yourself. Do you have a bias toward tasks or people?

Here are some prompts:

- If working from home, do you start your day connecting with others through social media?

- Do you make phone connections or meet up with a neighbor to start your day?

- Would you rather begin your day by sitting down and making a to-do list?

- Maybe you like to get organized first and even make a to-do list and check a few things off the list before you make a cup of coffee or tea.

 BUDDY UP This is also a great topic to talk with a buddy about later. Most of us lean toward one end of the continuum or the other. If you choose to talk with an accountability buddy instead of writing in a journal, that may give you an indication of your style!

Self-assess by putting a mark on the following line. Where do you think you fall in this continuum?

TASK-ORIENTED ——————————————————— **PEOPLE-ORIENTED**

PUT PACE AND PRIORITY TOGETHER

 JOT IT Look at the following simple chart and identify where you might fall. Circle the square that most accurately describes you.

	FAST	
Fast Pace Task-Oriented		Fast Pace People-Oriented
TASK-ORIENTED		**PEOPLE-ORIENTED**
Slow Pace Task-Oriented		Slow Pace People-Oriented
	SLOW	

SELF-AWARENESS IS A COMPETITIVE ADVANTAGE

Knowing yourself and your strengths, preferences, style, pace, and priorities is game-changing. Revealing personal behavioral patterns helps strengthen the foundation we build as we go along in this process.

The tool I use with clients is the DiSC assessment, which reveals our behavior preferences.

Based on the behavioral theory of psychologist William Marston, in his 1931 book, *DISC, Integrative Psychology*, Marston found four primary behavioral styles: Dominance, Influence, Steadiness, and Conscientiousness. Psychologists Walter Vernon Clarke and John Geier developed an assessment tool with these four behavioral styles as anchors. I use this tool in my practice because it offers a behavior-based lens and measures the malleable aspects. When we take a personality or IQ test, the results are static; we are born with a personality type. However, our behavior is something that can always change and evolve.[6]

 CLIENT PEEK

Once clients know their style, they can share insight with others so that there are no misinterpretations of behavior. For example, one of my clients practiced sharing his preference at the start of the meeting so that his listen-first style was not misinterpreted as agreement, not paying attention, or something else. The key is not letting others infer something incorrectly. So, he would casually comment at the start of meetings that he was eager to listen first to everyone's point of view; then, he would contribute his comments. This way, the fast-paced, active group would not think he was just going along with everything they shared.

Too Much: Be Careful with the Potential for Excess

We must be careful when utilizing an excess of our style, as too much of a good thing is often simply too much. Going fast may be too fast, or slowing down may get too slow. For a fast-paced leader, there may be a pattern of making more impulsive decisions that may have benefitted from further evaluation (I speak for myself here). Or, for those who take their time and read the fine print on every document just to be on the safe side, this style might end up missing opportunities. The key is to know yourself and your strengths. Remain open to the course correction needed if you find yourself in your personal style overuse mode. For greater group effectiveness, avoid pacing excesses. In the children's fable *The Tortoise and the Hare*, "slow and steady" wins the race. Sometimes, the tortoise needs a boost, and sometimes, the hare could practice at a more measured pace.

Hyperfocusing on tasks or people can also get us into trouble. Watch for this excess. I have coached clients on both sides and have some examples in the next Client Peek.

CLIENT PEEK

Taskmaster: After identifying that a senior leader was task-driven to excess, which was hurting his team because there was significant turnover, my client was open to establishing some new habits. He purposely posted a note on his door as a prompt to help him remember to say, "Hello, how was your weekend?" before jumping straight into tasks each week with his staff. He also willingly blocked time on his calendar on Monday mornings and Friday afternoons to make "rounds" at the office. Recognizing his preference for focusing on tasks, this leader acknowledged that other people he worked with might need more relationship-building, conversation, and connection than he needed.

People first. Many leaders claim to put people first. I worked with a client known as a fantastic people leader who often reminded her leadership team to put people first. As the business changed, this strength became an excess, and profitability became the most critical metric. She became known as the "softie" among her team members instead of being known for her business acumen and results. Changing her language to report more on data and becoming more vocal about results helped her rebalance her image in her company as a leader who works with people to create profitable outcomes.

Conflicts Often are Based on a Mismatch of Pace or Priority

If a conflict arises in a team, it is often related to misunderstandings based on pace and priority. I have too many examples to share where a leader might misinterpret a task-focused employee as being anti-social or a colleague focused on relationships to be evaluated poorly for wasting time, which is seen as socializing too much in the office. We must first understand our behavioral preferences and then be open to the differences in the workplace. Knowing yourself and having self-awareness is a competitive advantage. You will also begin to notice the preferences of the people around you and become even more effective with this awareness.

THE DISCOVER HALFWAY POINT: HALF THE BOAT IS BUILT

Take a minute to look back and see how much you have already put into this process. You are halfway there in the Discover phase. You have halfway left to go. Take a breath. You may want to look at yourself and evaluate your current state. You have already shared a lot regarding who you are today. We have also considered how people would describe you and how you would like them to describe you, which hints at the work of identifying who you want to become.

I typically take a moment to pause here and ask my clients what has resonated most from this conversation.

✎ **JOT IT**

- What is sticking with you? _____

_____

- What idea, goal, awareness, or energy is drawing your attention? _____

_____

This is a great time to talk to a buddy, use your journal, or even just look in the mirror.

Build your energy for the next chapter, as the second half of Discover lies just ahead.

Determining Your Future

You have just finished the first part of the Discover phase, which is exploring who you are now, a milepost for progress in this discovery section. The second part is looking to the future and defining what you want. We will accomplish this through some deep questions and topics to explore.

The work you do in this next section will serve you. This process is not easy or quick, but it is worth contemplating. These insights will help ground your decisions and behaviors for years to come. If this is your first time thinking about your identity, values, and what is most important to you, please take your time. Do not rush this foundational phase of the work.

WHO DO YOU WANT TO BE?

Now that we know our strengths and energy, the next essential step is to examine our identity. Our identity defines who we are and who we aspire to be. As kids, adults ask us, "What do you want to be when you grow up?" When asked this question, we separate who we are from who we may someday become. Even as kids, we can see this gap.

Seeing how many children take on their parents' career paths is always fascinating. For generations, parents have groomed their children to take on the trade they had learned. Often, competency, business acumen, and trade skills are learned from our parental role models.

I am also intrigued when doctors, actors, or other professionals say, "I would never want my child to choose this same path that I chose." Sometimes, parents' choices become the ones they hope their child avoids. As another example, many business owners would never want their children to take on the business.

From one generation to the next, humans evolved this way as skilled tradespeople or family lineage, inheriting the family profession from a young age and knowing the ropes by parental example. Do we have choices as we go? Once we choose a career path, we may coast along too long on cruise control. We may evolve into the person we were *expected* to become, only to crave more of the person we desire to be, doing the work that brings us fulfillment. We must make conscious choices as we determine who we are and what we do for a living. Those choices go well beyond the job we select and affect the quality of our lives.

Identity comprises beliefs, roles, priorities, and who we are. Our character is part of our identity. I enjoy hearing people describe their colleagues: "He is a great guy; everyone loves him" or "She's talented; she knows her stuff." Think about the first thing people might say when they describe you. Our identity will evolve as we grow; experiences shape us, and relationships influence it along the way.

What would you say if I asked you to share who you are and what you do? Does this introduction reflect what you hope to be known for? We sometimes get caught up in our job title, which does not often reflect the most meaningful elements of our identities. Consider your audience before introducing yourself. For example, if you are at a school event for your child, you might not say, "Hi, I'm CEO of X Corporation." Instead, you might introduce yourself as your child's father. So, consider the context for your introduction and how you think about yourself.

CLIENT PEEK

One practice I use with clients focused on clarifying their identity is to practice introductions. Each time I meet with that client, I ask them to introduce themselves to me, as if we are meeting for the first time. This practice might sound funny, but how we introduce ourselves reveals a lot about our current mindset and internal sense of identity. The words we select hold power. Since my clients are primarily business leaders at the top of their fields, I'm continually surprised when they use language that does not reflect the leader I see them to be. Often, leaders use their job titles in their first sentences when describing themselves. Consider this tendency for yourself. Do you first define yourself by your job, or is there another descriptor that comes to mind?

Let's look at all aspects of your identity as a starting point now. This is an excellent opportunity to use your journal and explore this.

 JOURNAL IT Here are some prompts to get you going:

- I am…

- I want to be known for…

Unhelpful Thoughts and Language

One thing that I never want to hear from anyone, including you, is "I am just a… (fill in the blank)." Using "just" detracts from who you are and what you do. Many women describe themselves as "just a stay-at-home mom," explaining they want to return to the workforce. When I had young kids and was fortunate to be with them for a play date or a music class, I remember thinking that many stay-at-home parents were the most active, taking their kids everywhere and never really staying home. It was an ironic descriptor.

Using certain labels to describe our identity is limiting. Some vocations align with our identity; I'm thinking of teachers, healthcare workers, and people whose job is to serve. However, most titles limit us to a narrow view of our identity based on what a corporation has hired us to do.

One of the most powerful things we can do is to define ourselves by the person we are to become, not our current job title.

WHAT ROLES DO YOU PLAY?

[handwritten note: Roles as it relates to others & what should those relationships look like.]

There are so many roles we play in life. Our roles attach to our identity. Many of us realize our identity consists of multiple descriptors. We all hold varied roles at certain times, with time allocated on our calendars every week dedicated to various positions. Sometimes, our work identity is prominent when we introduce ourselves to others. Most of my clients have an easy time defining their work roles. The roles that help us pay the bills are often easy to define—you might be an accountant or a sales leader or a retail manager. But we all have other roles that may not earn us money that we also play. You might be a mother, a father, a wife, a sister, a community organizer, a member of a religious group, a guitar player, or a good friend. Look back over your calendar for the past month. If you were taking meals to a neighbor who recently had surgery, picking up kids, or attending a family function for your sister…all these roles play a part in where we turn our time and attention. We look narrowly at our roles based on that primary job that keeps the lights on, pays the bills, and consumes most of our time.

When our lives evolve, we take on new roles. One of the most significant roles we may add is the title of "parent." Not everyone will take on this role. Yet even people who do not have children often have pets and parents and have similar experiences as primary caregivers. We might not consider how much these responsibilities shape our lives and how we spend our time. The key is ensuring our roles align with our values and intended identity. Sometimes, we do not choose these caregiver positions ourselves. These calls to action evolve throughout our lives. Being intentional about our roles helps curate a life with meaning and purpose.

Before we change anything, let's take inventory. Write down the roles you currently have in your life. Think about all the parts you have played in your life. Are you a leader, father, mother, sister, leader, volunteer Little League coach, caregiver, congregant, or teacher?

Consider your whole life. In the following chart, write down your role and, if helpful, a description of that role. Describe each function, especially if you wear multiple hats or have various forms of employment.

JOT IT

Role	Descriptor

WHAT DO YOU VALUE?

As we consider our identity, our roles, and who we want to become, the next step is to examine what we value. We are now penetrating the heart of the matter— essential for the foundation.

Of course, we all have some values in common. I am seeking your unique responses here, different from the expected values that everyone holds as essential. I want to know what *you* define as your most dearly held, necessary, and essential values. When I meet with clients, they often identify integrity as a top value. Most people want to act with integrity. I'm after the top three, four, or five values that define you, which are non-negotiable. Think about how you live and where you spend your time. Someone who works 75+ hours a week and hires an entire staff to care for the family members in their life might pick *ambition* and *security* instead of the word *family* as a more accurate foundational choice. Without judgment or second-guessing, simply look at your top values. Security might be more important to you than communication. Service might be more powerful for you than financial success. The words listed next are examples of values. Try not to qualify them. Let's just make sure you choose what resonates most for you.

JOT IT Circle three to four words.

Achievement, Ambition, Aesthetics, Artfulness, Belonging, Bravery, Calm, Caring, Consistency, Community, Compassion, Confidence, Conscientiousness, Consideration, Cooperation, Creativity, Courageousness, Decisiveness, Dependability, Determination, Diligence, Excellence, Enthusiasm, Exploration, Fairness Faith, Family, Fitness, Flexibility, Forgiveness, Generosity, Growth, Goodness, Giving, Happiness, Helpfulness, Honesty, Humbleness, Humor, Independence, Impartiality, Imagination, Intelligence, Joyfulness, Justice, Kindness, Love, Loyalty, Logic, Leadership, Maturity, Openness, Order, Patience, Patriotism, Peacefulness, Perseverance, Persistence, Positivity, Rationality, Reliability, Religion, Respect, Resourcefulness, Security, Self-Control, Service, Speed, Stability, Structure, Successfulness, Tact, Thankfulness, Thoroughness, Teamwork, Tolerance, Trustworthiness, Truthfulness, Usefulness, Versatility.

 JOT IT Pick values from this list or write descriptors that illuminate what you value most in your own words. Make it work for you, or create personalized additions:

- Value 1 _____

- Value 2 _____

- Value 3 _____

- Value 4 _____

Was it challenging to pick just a few? Did you wrestle with a couple of answers or want to extend your list? Are all four values you selected of equal importance to you? It is helpful to share your story about why you picked the values you did. This is a great time to use your tools—look in the mirror, connect with your accountability buddy, or pull out your journal.

 REFLECT It's time to return to the mirror. This exercise will help you get to know yourself by being honest and transparent.

 BUDDY UP Talking with a buddy might also help you clarify your values and explain the *why* behind each. Find a partner, spouse, friend, or mentor who can be a sounding board regarding why you chose these values.

People may suggest our values don't change throughout our lives. I disagree. I believe values evolve as our roles evolve. Perhaps ambition and creating wealth might come before family when we are young and single. Or after facing a serious health diagnosis, adventure and seeing the world might climb on the list. Early experiences shape some values, and I can attest to that. I have had many clients share with me that they chose "security" as their primary value and that this value originated for them in their childhood. It is helpful to explore the origin of why you think you might have picked the values you did.

ARE YOU LIVING IN LINE WITH OUR VALUES?

Once we discuss our values, the big question becomes—are we living in line with these values? What stands in the way of us living our lives aligned with these values? Are our values reflected in our daily or weekly activities? Look at your calendar from last week or last month. Do you see evidence of activities and commitments that support your values?

Consider the roles you identified for yourself. Is there one missing? Do you need to get involved with something new or take on a project or activity that reflects a value you hold dear?

 CLIENT PEEK

A client was passionate about participating in community service in her city. She had been actively involved in service events, but after a demanding job promotion, she could no longer commit to volunteering. We discussed all she had on her plate and her roles and then compared her various role commitments with her values. She realized that with her 70-hour workweek she could not continue with some of her commitments. We brainstormed ways to keep the commitment to the value while changing her direct role. She shifted this voluntary role, gave the spot to another community member, and then developed a program to bring community members monthly into her business and assist them with their careers at her office instead.

Do you have any roles that are out-of-date with your values? Have you been part of a team or a group at work since you started that you may have outgrown? For example, you might be a school committee member, and this role requires a time commitment. You may have enjoyed several years working as a volunteer on that committee. You have developed new interests, and rather than working on that same committee, you may choose something more directly aligned with other values.

Look for outdated roles where you are going through the motions and recognize that it might be time to move on from a role. Pick something new that will fill you with energy and purpose, directly in line with your values.

Asking Yourself the Big Questions!

Answering the following two questions is the final step in our discovery process. They are critical to determining who you want to become, so answer the questions thoughtfully.

- Why do you work? _____

- What does success look like?_____

The answers to these questions have been the most powerful in generating helpful discussions for my work with clients. Let's take one at a time.

WHY DO YOU WORK?

Why people work runs deep. The most obvious answer is "to make money," yet I rarely get that answer from my clients. Money is a significant factor in why people work, and "to provide for my family" is a standard answer. Yet, this is where the possibilities begin to bubble up—we have many ways of making income as we journey through life. The key is to align our way of earning income to the things that bring us the most fulfillment and are most in line with what we value. We can see countless examples of people taking on work as a means to a different end besides "making money."

Sometimes, I hear clients' stories from childhood, first jobs, or chores at home as a young child. Instilled values from clients' upbringing—the environment or conditions in which they drew meaning from young childhood to teenagers— have shaped their initial work ethic formation.

We all have choices about what to do for work, no matter what point of life we are in presently. Sometimes, our choices are limited, but we often have options, even if they are tough. Consider why you work.

A Quick Review of Maslow's Hierarchy of Needs

You may say, "Why I work is because I need to work." However, let us look at the psychology behind our needs to consider as we answer why we work.

American psychologist Abraham Maslow introduced a pyramid to illustrate the hierarchy of human needs. As shown here, basic needs must come first. Basic needs, at the base of the pyramid, are physiological needs; they are things we need to stay alive: food, a place to live, water. They are the essentials. Without them, we cannot continue up the pyramid. Once these are satisfied, we can look to the next level up in the pyramid and focus on our job choices.[7]

Maslow's Hierarchy of Needs

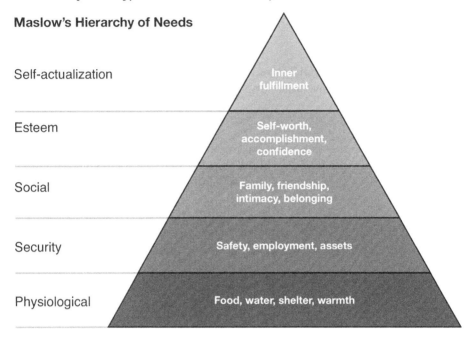

Self-actualization	Inner fulfillment
Esteem	Self-worth, accomplishment, confidence
Social	Family, friendship, intimacy, belonging
Security	Safety, employment, assets
Physiological	Food, water, shelter, warmth

Think back on how it felt when you became an adult and began to make a living for yourself. In these early years, we have a straightforward answer to why we work. We must pay for food, shelter, and utilities. We must work to cover the basics. Perhaps this is your current phase of life now.

On the other end of life experience, I have also worked with many leaders who tell me right up front that they do not have to work (anymore). They share that they choose to work and stay in the workforce later in life as it provides a purpose for them. Meet your physiological needs, and you can move up the pyramid and eventually toward self-actualization.

WHY DO YOU WORK? I AM ASKING AGAIN!

Many of us still have a lot of years left to work. As a society, we are working progressively later in our lives. So, with that long life ahead of us, clarifying why we work is essential. At some point in your work life, I hope you achieve the needs closer to the top of the pyramid—esteem and self-actualization. Navigating the pyramid takes time; everyone has different circumstances. The goal, however, would be for you to meet your physiological needs so that your work becomes a choice to fulfill the pyramid's social, esteem, and self-actualized tiers.

If you, like most of us, have to work, consider why you work in your current role or employer and think more broadly about why you picked this particular position for this phase of your life. What does this employment provide you beyond the paycheck? Consider reflecting on and answering this question in as much detail as possible.

 JOT IT or **JOURNAL IT** Why do you work? Right now, or for the next three to five years ahead?

If you are fortunate enough to "not have to work," I hope you still contemplate your answers to this question. Provide all the ideas that pertain to your current life. Take some time to sit with this question and respond here or in your journal.

> In her 2022 book *The Nowhere Office,* Julia Hobsbawm looks at the evolution of work and defines distinct phases of work life. She notes that many people started questioning why they work during the COVID-19 pandemic, and she notes there were major shifts in how people work. She writes, "It is not surprising at a time of dramatic change that more people are asking why they work and what it means."[8]

No matter what phase you are in your life, it is essential to reflect on why you work to ensure you are not living with outdated assumptions from your past answers to this question. So, I am nudging you now to answer this question.

WHAT DOES SUCCESS LOOK LIKE TO YOU IN THIS MOMENT?

This next essential question ties back to the previously outlined values; consider your values when answering this. Please take the time to answer this new question fully. This inquiry will require more than a one-sentence answer.

We live in a society where we receive a barrage of messages not specifically tailored to each of us as individuals. Social media leads us to believe that bigger is better, success is the norm, and most people are always living their best lives. You may start to wonder if everyone owns a yacht! Yet this filtered fantasy is rarely the case.

These external messages add noise and distraction to our internal thinking and challenge our beliefs. As self-actualized humans, we don't need advertising firms or travel agencies telling us what we aspire to. Take control! Define success very personally for yourself.

JOT IT Personalize your vision of success.

What does success look like for you?_____

_____

_____

 BUDDY UP This is a great question to answer with someone important in your life. You could also pose this question to them and listen to their answers. We should also know the answers for people we work with, especially if they are on your staff. We should explore our spouse's response to this question or a partner's or best friend's reply. If we know what we define as success, we will know when we get there.

SUCCESS COMES WHEN?

Since we each define success differently, we must set expectations for ourselves. This question is one that you need to ask yourself throughout the stages of your life. Success for a college student might be to graduate within a timeframe. Success for a front-line manager might be retaining their employees and contributing to accomplishing the company goals. Success for an executive might be performing their best at work while having the freedom to spend their time as they choose. Form a clear vision of what success looks like because if you leave it nebulous or undefined, you will never have the satisfaction of getting there. If we keep moving the goal line, we will never arrive.

Discover Highlights

Your answers to all of the previous questions have laid the foundation. Discover is the essential first step in the 4D process, and it sets you up for success for all future work. Think about the discovery phase you just completed as the effort of building the hull of a seaworthy boat. The *hull* is the term for the actual body of a ship; it is the watertight enclosure that protects the cargo, people, and supplies. The hull must be strong, stable, and seaworthy in building any functional vessel. Through your commitment to carefully answering all of the questions in this section, you have prepared the most robust boat for inevitable surprising weather or whitecaps on the unpredictable, rocky seas ahead.

Completing the discovery foundation should bring you some feeling of accomplishment. Very little can hold you back when you have the mindset of change—a philosophy of growth, abundance, possibility, and confidence. Take a minute to celebrate *you*. When a boat's construction has been realized, it is customary to christen the vessel before its first journey. Breaking a bottle of champagne over the boat's bow is said to bring good luck for travel ahead. I hope you will take a few moments to acknowledge your handy work. Your hull's frame was crafted with intent. Celebrate!

Your boat's hull, the discover stage, has given you the resources to take future trips and arrive at exciting destinations. What an accomplishment to have built this solid foundation. Next, use the efforts of your labor to reach greater and greater desired goals. Don't forget you are your own best captain.

Strengths _____

Preferences _____

Style _____

Why You Work _____

Success _____

Values _____

You

Sturdy Foundation The hull of your
ship for this journey

 ## Discover: Key Takeaways

Let's make sure that we take action to create the life we want and move toward that life starting today. You can capture the discoveries in this section. Place your answers to the following questions on the planks of your boat's hull above.

- What are your strengths to capture?

- What brings you energy? What are your preferences?

- What is your style: fast/slow and task/people?

- Why do you work?

- What does success look like—your vision—for you?

- What are your top values?

PHASE 2: DECIDE

Identifying and Committing to a Target

We've arrived at the next phase in our process. It's time to decide. Since you spent time building a safe and sturdy boat, you can now decide where to go on that boat. This decision can be specific. Now, we will identify what you want your next destination to be.

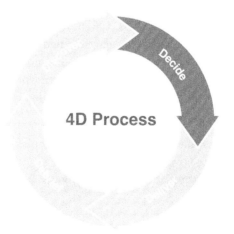

You worked hard to build your seafaring hull, and through this, you may have shifted or expanded your focus. Your ship is sturdy and well-built. We can travel further than perhaps you initially thought.

We will approach this next leap by starting with an extensive view and then narrowing things down and getting specific. Using our boat analogy, we will start by identifying some possible destinations. With a desire to travel into unknown waters, we can start by making a wish list. You might pick a far-flung position, a dream job in Iceland, or a cozy cove along the West Coast to dock until the conditions are ideal to launch again. Later in this process, we will zero in on choosing the most desirable destination. But we have considerations to make for this phase of our journey together. How is the weather? Are there any storms on the horizon? What is our budget, and what time of year can we make such an ambitious trip? Who will we select as crew members on this voyage?

Now is the time to capitalize on your new awareness and energy from your discovery work. Let's go, decide what is next, and then make change happen! Using your fresh discovery of your values, strengths, and all you have uncovered, we will revisit your vision for what is next.

Envisioning Your Success

Think about one year from today. One year from today's date—to be exact—let's focus solely on that. What would make the most significant difference? What would it look like if you focused on one aspect of a substantial change over the following year?

In my experience, the big questions in Discover get us to a new place. Sometimes, a client will tell me in our first meeting that they want to stop doing what they are doing, quit, retire, or change careers. Often, it is all in or all out, and it is a big decision to make. Frequently, they have defined their next steps from a narrowed perspective based on their current options, not what they want to incorporate into their lives. After we do the discovery work, look at their values, and review why they work, they decide to try something different and usually take off in a newly discovered direction.

Revisit the presenting problem or the reason that you picked up this book to make a change. Consider now what your definition of success is, why you work, and how your values inform that issue. Is it changing? Has your original scope expanded?

JOT IT You might have started with a problem you are trying to solve, and now you may be rethinking whether you have the right job at this point in your life. You might want to start a new hobby or take on a new role in your life based on your discovery work. Before going further, we need to get even more precise and decide what we are trying to achieve. Let's revisit the initial questions.

- What is the problem you want to solve? _____

- What is the outcome you envision? _____

- Why must you have this goal accomplished? _____

Before we get practical about the particulars, let's make a wish list. Try not to edit yourself, at least not right away. You already know why you picked up this book; now, understanding your initial motivation and your new awareness, let's continue.

DEVELOP A WORKING VISION

 JOT IT Start big, and do not critique yourself. Here are some prompts. Feel free to write whatever comes to mind.

- Who do you want to be in one year? _____

- What do you want to be doing? _____

- Where do you want to be living and working? _____

- Who do you want to have in your life? _____

There are many paths toward the journey itself. If we recognize and embrace our desires, we may spend a lifetime deciding how much further we can reach. I am not pressuring you about where you want to be 10 years from now. I find this approach to be much more practical. Think about what you want to accomplish, avoid, get, fix, or do in the next six months. We are gearing up for action, moving out of the reflection stage, and picking our destination.

JOT IT Describe Yourself in Six Months or One Year from Today

_____

_____

_____

_____

 JOURNAL IT As always, if you want more time or more space for these important questions, pull out your journal or

 BUDDY UP Ask a buddy to discuss the questions in further detail.

DETERMINE THE *WHY* BEHIND YOUR GOAL

Why does this goal matter to you? What will you gain? What will you avoid?

The *why* test is part of the specific goal discussed previously. We will take another look to ensure your plans are clear and directly connected to your *why*.

Just as we looked at your *why* for engaging in this process at the start of this work, be sure to continually check in with yourself to clarify why you are setting a specific goal. The *why* will keep us motivated and on track.

Getting a promotion, for example, sounds like a powerful goal, and clarifying the *why* behind it will help. Suppose you want to get to the next-level job in your corporation so that you can begin to save money for a house or your children's college fund; that lends to a more powerful *why*. Name something you can see creating a benefit that aligns with your core values and what is most important to you now.

Let's not let the *why* be murky or nebulous. One example of a health goal that many relate to is a goal to lose weight. The initial *why* behind this might be "to get healthier," but it is not so specific. It may be difficult to credit the results of slightly better blood work as making any difference in your life. Yet, there is more meaning attached to incremental change if you choose the *why* to match directly with your values. If you want to lose weight to live longer for your family, that is powerful. Explore your specific vision; it may be to get on the floor to play with your child (or grandchild) or climb around on the playground equipment to maintain a playful relationship and close bond with those same children. As you can you see, that is an example of a powerful *why*!

Whether your goal is related to work or your personal life, make it meaningful and clear.

 REFLECT Take a minute to reflect on your *why*.

Setting Some Goals

We have visualized success, and now we want to achieve that vision. The best way to close the gap from where you are today to where you'd like to be is by deciding what you want to do to get there. It's time to determine what we will focus on and what is less critical. Let's set some new *goals*!

Setting goals, writing them down, reviewing the visual evidence of our progress, and managing the progress toward an accomplishment will give us some direction, not to mention long-lasting benefits. Writing goals takes a few passes; clients usually take three specific times to write, refine, and confirm their goals. As a coach, one of my most significant contributions to clients is to act as a sounding board for the task of defining their goals. I want you to feel that you can accomplish what you set out to achieve and that you set goals to genuinely improve your life.

So, using this energy, let's define some goals. Write down one, two, or three goals here. We will test them, refine them, and edit them later. For now, simply capture your thinking in a first draft of one to three primary goals.

✎ JOT IT

1. _____

2. _____

3. _____

WHY WE SET GOALS

Is goal setting worth the effort? Yes! Setting goals leads to achievement, gives us direction, and gives us the feeling of accomplishment, which motivates us to do more to achieve those goals. This cycle repeats, and the more often we set goals, the more reinforced success we experience, and the more we crave another goal.

Setting Goals Leads to Achievement

A quick internet search reveals many studies that claim that writing down our goals sets us up to achieve them. Studies report that we are 42% more likely to accomplish a goal if it is written down, than if we do not write them. Consequently, we will focus on setting goals and writing them down to increase our odds of achieving our vision. You already took a first pass. You will soon have another opportunity to refine your goal.

Setting Goals Provide Us with Direction

Goals give us something to strive for. Realizing a dream is not necessarily the end point of accomplishment as much as the encouragement and validation needed to embark on the next journey. Learning new ways of approaching our goals and systematic habit formation brings us closer to the person we want to become.

Setting Goals Gives Us the Feeling of Accomplishment

Accomplishing the things we set out to do is fantastic and fulfilling. The following sequential steps will yield unforeseen benefits and increase your motivation.

One of my favorite quotes, attributed to Norman Vincent Peale, is, "Shoot for the moon. Even if you miss, you'll land among the stars."[9] Set your goal out *there*, and your trajectory for greatness will span further than you may have thought possible.

If we set goals and accomplish them, we also benefit from the feeling of that accomplishment. I don't know if you paid attention in biology class, but accomplishment provides a physiological change in our bodies by releasing endorphins. When you accomplish a goal or check a task off your list, your body's natural reward system releases endorphins. Some people may write something they have already accomplished on their to-do list just for the bliss of crossing it off. Endorphins can help reduce stress, help with pain management, and give a general euphoric feeling. In a subsequent chapter, we address sustaining health habits and discuss other ways to release endorphins. There are many tried-and-tested ways of tricking the brain's reward center and releasing more positive feelings. For now, consider working on your goals so that you benefit from that pleasurable feeling of accomplishing them.

HOW MANY GOALS TO SET

Do not let the number of goals overwhelm you. I often must remind myself of this mantra: "We do not have to accomplish everything on a Monday." To set ourselves up for success, keep it simple. Pick one, two, or three goals to commit to. The feeling of accomplishing one or two goals will fuel our commitment to continuing this process.

The last thing I want is for you to grow frustrated with too many goals and priorities simultaneously. This overwhelming feeling may prompt us to drop the goals all at once and promote feelings of failure. With your values in mind, your clear definition of what success looks like right now, and great answers for why you work, consider something specific you can commit to and will work on over the next several months. Is this what you wrote earlier? We have another chance to take a pass at this.

Many of us tend to pile on goals at certain times of year—New Year's resolutions come to mind. I recently met with someone who had set up some health goals at the start of the year. As it turned out, he decided to try to get healthy, so he cut out alcohol. Then he also mentioned he was not eating carbs, had stopped smoking, was trying to get to the gym as much as he could, and more. He was so focused on a timeline for this cleanse and was counting down the days until he could return to alcohol, carbs, smoking, and his prior lifestyle. This is not what I recommend for your goal setting. The goals we pick can help us evolve into the person we aspire to be, not serve as a countdown to returning to our old habits and lifestyle. The goals we discuss will move you forward and get you closer to the person you are becoming. Ideally, there will be new habits we will incorporate into our lifestyle for years to come.

Listen to yourself carefully. What goal would make the most impact in your life? What difference could you make if you focused solely on this one thing over the next six months? Be a witness to what resonates.

Is there one goal you can identify as your ultimate goal that would yield success in all areas of your life? If so, pick that!

In *Good to Great,* Jim Collins coined the term *Big, Hairy, Audacious Goal* (BHAG) to describe one ultimate goal that connects passion, economic value, and being the best in the world at something. He describes this greatness as a "huge and daunting goal—like a big mountain to climb." This acronym is both clear and compelling. While Collins refers to the BHAG in a corporate context, we can also use it in general goal setting. Collins suggests that we keep things simple. He writes, "The key elements of greatness are deceptively simple and straightforward. The good-to-great leaders were able to strip away so much noise and clutter and just focus on the few things that would have the greatest impact."[10] Do not get too wrapped up in the clutter and noise. Instead, get quiet and go back to the mirror. Pick a powerful goal that will help your life improve.

WHEN YOU KNOW GOALS ARE COMPLETE

Now that you have taken the first pass at achieving your goals, let's ensure they are complete.

We need to put them through a couple of tests: the SMART Test and the Excitement Test. You may be familiar with the criteria for evaluating goals that I use in my sessions with clients. I want to ensure they are SMART goals you feel compelled to achieve.

The SMART Test

SMART covers all the bases. The more specific the goal is, the easier it will be to evaluate if you have accomplished it. If you set a goal to "be healthier this next year," this is too vague of a plan. We will never know how to evaluate your progress. Instead, be as specific as you can be. Your defined goal will prompt tangible success. Likewise, adding measures to make the goal relevant, attainable, and time-bound will make sure your goal is complete.

SMART goals are

- **Specific**: What exactly will you do, and why?

- **Measurable**: How will you know when you have achieved it? What measures can you see?

- **Attainable**: Goals within reach are achievable. I am not suggesting you make goals easy or simplified. Set realistic expectations to accomplish the goal.

- **Relevant**: The goal is aligned with your values and who you want to become.

- **Time-Based**: Defines when you will accomplish your goal and sets your deadline.

Here are some examples of making your goal aligned with the SMART criteria:

Vague	SMART
"Get promoted"	"Take on two new projects in the next six months to show my value to the leadership team."
"Be healthier this next year"	"Take 10,000 steps six days a week for the next six months."
"Network more"	"Schedule 3 meetings a week with new contacts and follow up with them to build relationships over the next two months."
"Eating healthier this next year"	"Add leafy greens to one meal a day for the following year."

✎ **JOT IT** Let's test some of your goals against the SMART criteria so that you get familiar with this approach. Write your goal here, and then evaluate it.

My goal: _____

_____

Is my goal:

Specific	○ Yes	○ No	**Relevant**	○ Yes	○ No
Measurable	○ Yes	○ No	**Time-Based**	○ Yes	○ No
Attainable	○ Yes	○ No			

The Excitement Test

We have internal and external motivation; external motivation only goes so far, accomplishing so much. To be great, we need that intrinsic motivation to drive real change and improvement. And for this mindset, both belief in yourself and enthusiasm must be present.

Intrinsic motivation, the kind that comes from within, is the motivation we discuss in this process. Looking back, you defined what success looks like, identified your *why*, and built the foundation. Your *why* should be the anchor for your motivation. Your goal should excite you and maybe even scare you a little bit.

CLIENT PEEK

When working with a long-term client, I was privileged to meet with this leader and her team to discuss the absence of women at the C level, in other words, at the top leadership level of their company. As a group, we agreed it would be excellent if a woman were in one of these leadership positions. Quickly, my call-to-action style prompted me to suggest to my client that we should all support her growth and efforts, and she should be the first female leader on this senior team. What an exciting statement and vision, for me, at least. After this lunch, we all were digesting this idea and wondered if any action might be taken toward this vision. It was clear that no matter what I said, this leader had to dig deep herself and identify if this was something that she wanted, something she felt motivated to accomplish. It truly took internal motivation and a personal belief from the leader herself. Once she shared her motivation, we were able to outline a plan for how she would navigate this career advancement with detailed steps. I was privileged to be her guide as she was able to build the motivation, confidence, and competence to rise to the most senior level of her company two years after this lunch discussion.

There is a difference between capability and motivation. If you are a manager, you know from experience that some employees are eager to jump on a task or project with positive attitudes while others are not. Or, if you have raised a child or influenced a younger sibling, you most likely know the challenge of trying to motivate a toddler. Getting an unwilling child to put their shoes on, even if they are fully capable of the task or any daily activity, is often challenging. You have probably heard the saying "You can lead a horse to water, but you cannot make them drink." That is what I am talking about here. How do we lead by example and inspire our sometimes stubborn (inner horse) self?

As one of the driving forces behind our behavior, there is some mystery about why some people muster up more motivation than others. Let's face your current motivation.

 REFLECT Take a hard look in the mirror.

- Do you still feel the energy and excitement to get started, or has the initial energy for this process faded by now?

- Are you ready to face this goal?

- Do you see the reflection in the mirror of a person who has the capacity to accomplish this goal? What would that person look like?

Be honest with yourself about your excitement and motivation to accomplish your goals.

In his popular book *Outliers*, Malcolm Gladwell's research states that it takes approximately 10,000 hours to become an expert in something. Yet, we still can't qualify why one child might spend years playing with LEGOs with a single pointed focus on honing a talent for building and spatial awareness, while another child might want to play hockey one day and try baseball or diving the next, switching their concentration up as fast as the seasons change. We can see examples of professional athletes who have dedicated their time and energy to one specific sport. If all conditions are right, such as their body composition, their financial ability to fund their sports interest, their parent's willingness to schlep them to practice and games, geography, etc., they may achieve success. However, there is no direct link between intention, willingness, and actual outcomes. Yet, we know for sure that internal motivation plays an essential role in making things happen.

Consider where and when you feel motivated and determine why you might need a nudge.

GOALS THAT REFLECT YOUR CHOICES AND MOTIVATION

Is it rare to be able to think about your day ahead and ask yourself, "What do I *want* to do? I have the whole day open. I'm as free as free can be." Instead, most of us wake up and consider our long to-do list for the day ahead. Our responsibilities and relationships fill our calendars with obligations we "have to do." These are the scheduled things we think we must do each and every day.

Now consider our life, our opportunity. When setting our goals, this should be a chance for us to identify what we want to do versus what we "should" do or have to do. We make incremental changes that will lead us in the direction we want it to go. Sometimes, we get hung up on a chosen path and take on things we must do. I get it. We all have responsibilities and bills to pay. You can say "I choose to" or "I get to" to remind your brain that we have the freedom of choice. Certainly, there are consequences related to choices, such as whether we learn early in school or live in our parents' home. You suffer the consequences if you choose not to do homework or decide not to obey a curfew. Let's be clear that we continually strive to own our choices in life.

Viktor Frankl's book *Man's Search for Meaning* is the ultimate example of our freedom of choice. In 1945, Frankl wrote about the horrors of the Nazi camps, providing the reader with some profound clarity about the power of our mindset. The only thing he had left in the concentration camps in Nazi Germany aside from his life was his freedom to choose.

"We who lived in concentration camps can … offer sufficient proof that everything can be taken from a man but one thing: the last of the human freedoms—to choose one's attitude in any given set of circumstances, to choose one's own way."[11]

I am hopeful that your life circumstances as you read these pages are not dire and that you firmly believe that your future is yours to create. I often hear clients list things they just have to do, as if there is no choice in the matter, when, in fact, they have total control over their choices and actions. So, keep this in mind as we continue to evaluate goals. Let us use language that reflects what we get to do or choose to do. To live, we must make choices; if we are fortunate enough to have choices, let's make decisions with our eyes open.

Setting Yourself Up for Achieving Your Goals

Think deeply about your vision of your future. Your goals should help you create the life you want. Here are a few more tools to help set up for goal achievement.

ENSURE YOUR GOALS ALIGN WITH THE LIFE YOU WANT

Our first helpful reminder is to step back and look at the big picture. Rather than sharply focusing on your specific goal, or slice of the pie so to speak, think about the whole pie. Having a work-related goal is great, something like: "I want to be promoted this year to the next level at work," yet let's look at that goal in the context of your whole life.

In Cheryl Richardson's *Take Time for Your Life,* she used a pie graphic to outline all of the pieces that make up our lives. At the time, this book helped bring the concept of "work-life balance" into corporate discussions. In 2024, employers are well aware that their workforce will have an interest in looking at their whole life regarding their time allocation, not just their work life.

This pie chart introduced the concept of thinking about your whole life, not just your career. Having a visual resonates with my clients, and here is a pie that I created as a starting point for you to customize:

The key is to make this pie your own and detail each slice.

- Is there a vital category missing?

- Do you need to separate physical health and mental health?

- Do you want family time as a different piece of the pie from relationships?

Customize this pie to your needs, with your language. There is an opportunity to represent your current life and then design your future. Identify the categories that must be described and use the language that resonates most for you. Think back to the roles that you identified. These roles may translate directly to the pie. Reference your notes like quality ingredients for delicious pie!

As you draw your customized pie chart next, consider how big some sections are currently and how big you would like each slice to be in the future. What piece of the pie will be the most significant slice in one year? Is this assumption based on your definition of what is most important or where you spend most of your time? Consider creating a pie for your vision one year from today that accurately reflects the priority for each slice. Your pie does not need to be balanced, with each section claiming the same amount of your time; rather, each section should represent the desired amount of time in your daily schedule.

Some of these slices may be more important for you now than others, based on your life phase, current career, and the elements themselves. Do not judge yourself; get creative and select specific categories that tell your story of the life you want to lead. Complete the following pie charts to support your vision for your future.

JOT IT Fill these in for yourself.

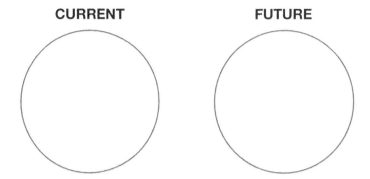

New Role?

Once you complete the pie, ask yourself—is there a new role I need to take on in my life to accomplish this goal? If you have a slice that is not represented by a role in your life, consider this now and think about how you can add it. If service, for example, is important to you and you do not currently have a role in your community, it is time to look for a place to volunteer. If you want to strengthen your image at work as someone well-known in the marketplace, you may need to get a role on a board or join a trade association or chamber of commerce. Think about the functions you have had and if they will enable you to realize that future vision for yourself.

USE VISUAL CUES AS TOOLS

The pie is an example of a visual cue, and visual cues can be compelling. Other examples are a vision board, a calendar with days crossed off when you worked toward a specific purpose or a short list of things to accomplish in the month ahead.

What do you have hanging on the walls of your workspace? Diplomas or certifications? Do you have inspirational statements with photos or paintings depicting uplifting scenes? Do you have any visual way to track your progress toward accomplishing your goals? Creating a scorecard or a dashboard to measure, monitor, and track your progress may also be helpful. Place and personalize your visual cues to pull you back into your intended outcome.

Creating a Vision Board

If you like visual cues, take a little time to create a vision board. If you haven't heard of a vision board, it is a physical representation of goals or aspirations. You can take a big poster board or a corkboard or get creative and make something unique. On this board, you can creatively illustrate:

- Goals—things you want to accomplish

- Intentions—for example, more patience with yourself, a partner, or a child

- Dreams/wishes— a new home, a dream vacation, something you aspire to

- Phrases or mantras—remind your inner voice how you prefer *you* speak to you (for example: "We're ready to begin! Let's get started! Be mindful").

I keep a big calendar in my office with work commitments and family activities, and next to that, I have my vision board. I sometimes take the big cardboard blotter from my desk calendar and create a vision board for the upcoming year ahead. You can look through magazines, take photos, or even write words or phrases for this. Get creative and have fun with this.

A Picture Is Worth (a Thousand?) Words

Forbes reports research that vividly describes that goals are more likely to be accomplished with visual aids. "Vividly describing your goals in written form is strongly associated with goal success, and people who very vividly describe or picture their goals are anywhere from 1.2 to 1.4 times more likely to successfully accomplish their goals."[12]

Writing Your Goals Down and Tracking Their Progress

 JOURNAL IT Just writing down our goals signals our brain! If we write down our goals, we are more likely to accomplish them! What an influence. This is why you have so many chances here to write your goals. Need another reason to write these down?

If we write down all the tasks we need to accomplish our goals, we benefit from checking them off the list. For example, if you set up a goal of writing an article and completing the piece, you feel great when you finally hand it off to the editor.

IMPLEMENT POSITIVE TALK/INNER VOICE

We all can use encouragement to accomplish our goals. There is never a bad time for positive self-talk. Some people are more comfortable with this practice than others. Do you prefer recognition from other people? Or are you someone who relies on your own voice? Your journal is a forever tool to talk yourself through new and improved internal dialogue. A journal can also become a barometer to reveal what's happening inside you. Use your reflections as a correspondence between yourself and your written thoughts, and use the mirror for positive affirmations. People who are kind with their inner voices are more likely to succeed.

Here are some great phrases to try if you aren't familiar with positive self-talk:

- "I have prepared; I can do this!"

- "I have got you, and you've got this!"

- "This project is in your wheelhouse; you are capable!"

- "I am going to rock this presentation!"

 JOURNAL IT Take a minute to capture what language works best for you in your journal.

Psychology Today and other mainstream publications have documented that positive self-talk can influence various potential outcomes. We know that professional sports teams and athletes have used this method to boost performance for years. "A 2020 study of three 800-meter runners found evidence that using self-talk made them run faster and feel mentally tougher. Their performances spoke for themselves."[13]

Implementing this practice sounds like common sense; telling ourselves that we can accomplish our goal helps our brain believe anything is possible. However, telling ourselves that we stink, are worthless, and cannot accomplish anything would have the opposite effect. If we have a negative bias in our brain that gives us critical messages, it may be detrimental to our well-being, not to mention our overall effectiveness.

If you have been preconditioned by a lifetime of critical internal comments, the easiest thing to do when facing a negative thought or criticism is to flip the script, reverse the present narrative, and train yourself to think the complete opposite of what you hear yourself saying. Using the opposite rhetoric, you can use the exact language but rearrange negative self-concepts. It is our job to reverse these negative messages. Anything is possible; give yourself the benefit of that positive self-talk! This is a habit that you can break if you are someone who starts with negative self-talk. It is time to make a habit of positive self-talk!

FLIP THE SCRIPT: Change your Negative to a Positive

Negative	Positive
I will never bring a new client to our business.	I *am* good enough to bring a new client into our business; just watch me.
I am not good enough to get the promotion.	Each day, I can improve, and sometime soon, I will get the promotion.
Why would anyone pick me for the project?	I would be an asset to the team in helping with this project.
My choices have not been great, and I am stuck in a job that I don't even like.	Starting today, I can make better choices, and I have the power to find a job that inspires me and values my contributions.

 REFLECT You can try your own language in the mirror right now!

One of my favorite things to remind clients is that when we know better, we do better. We are works in progress. We are constantly learning and evolving. Often, I hear my clients label themselves as bad at something. Language is powerful! Changing the language to the positive is helpful. The phrase I really like to use is "I am becoming."

Some quick examples include the following:

- "I am becoming a leader that provides feedback to my team."

- "I am becoming a better listener."

- "I am becoming someone who is on time for most things."

Consider your *why* and what you are becoming. Give this language a try.

MANIFEST YOUR FUTURE *How do. clients React to manifestation?*

It has become more mainstream to think of "putting things out into the universe" or "manifesting" something—like attracts like!

The basic philosophy of manifesting is that if you put something out into the universe, wish for it, visualize it, pray for it, or repeatedly think about it, the thought will attract a desired outcome. While I love that our universe has an energy we cannot entirely measure or see with the naked eye, manifesting might also involve planning and hard work. Luck and fate are certainly forces to consider when accomplishing a goal; hard work often pays off, too. So, manifest, visualize, hope, dream, and write down your goals.

Many of the clients that I have worked with report back to me that once they say something out loud, it seems to manifest. So take the time to say things out loud, put things into the universe, and create visual representations of your goals. Sharpening your picture of your future is certainly a helpful step to making it a reality.

"A goal is a dream with a deadline," said Napoleon Hill.[14] It's time to transform your dreams into reality. This forward momentum is powerful, as we tend to stay in motion when we are in motion. So, let's keep moving forward and work toward accomplishing our goals.

TAKE A FINAL PASS AT YOUR GOALS

This is your final opportunity to lock down your working goal(s) for this process. If you have not written anything down yet, this is your chance! If you have been following along diligently in the process, this is the final edit, the finishing touch. In the spaces coming up next, take the time to confirm your decisions so far.

- Look back at the initial answers you provided for where you want to be in one year.

- Now consider the pie you created and the big picture.

- Think deeply about who you want to be and what your identity will be in the year ahead.

CREATE YOUR PERSONAL ACTION PLAN

Now that you have chosen one meaningful goal, we need to round this out and define the *how* action plans to get this goal accomplished.

When I work with clients on their business goals, we often consider a one-year timeframe. The annual review is often a place where goals are measured, but six months out works, too. These are helpful timeframes to consider when writing your goal.

Once we have mapped our big goal, we can break down action items to attain what we have set out to do. We call this creating the action plan. Consider the following client example.

⬚ CLIENT PEEK

A client was eager to bring in a new "deal" for his company, and he knew there were many ways to achieve this. The overarching goal was to:

Bring in a specific dollar amount deal and establish a new client relationship in the year ahead.

While this is a great goal, it is specific, measurable, relevant, and time-based. He also needed to identify how to achieve the goal and what steps he would take to accomplish it.

So, he set a specific parameter for the big goal: "*Bring in a deal worth at least $X this calendar year.*"

Then, we worked on the *elements within that goal* that he would need to focus on, all assessed against the SMART criteria:

- Attend one marketing event/ industry event or a meal with a potential client each week.

- Publish one article every other month on LinkedIn or in a trade journal.

- Practice asking for a deal at each monthly meeting with my coach.

- Sharpen my elevator pitch to be easy and repeatable, and practice saying a 30-second pitch each week (with a buddy or my coach).

- Practice my "close" and "pitch" each quarter with a partner in the firm.

- Learn the specifics around contracts to execute a new deal with the proper paperwork by month 2.

The big goal is to bring in a new deal, and the subgoals and action items are also specific, measurable, time-based, relevant, and attainable.

This is it! Select one or two goals to commit to now and then define the action steps here:

Your Goal with Action Steps

My goal I will focus on in the next six months: _____

_____

JOT IT My action steps to meeting this goal:

Specific Action Items	How Measured	Related To/ Contingent On	By When

Decide Highlights

Decide is when we get laser-focused on one, two, or three goals and commit to achieving them. We have put them through the tests, and we have considered the whole pie in our goal setting. Writing down goals helps us commit to them and sharing them with a buddy strengthens our resolve to make them happen. We can revisit the Decide phase, setting more goals in the future as needed. Keep your self-talk positive and you are on your way to reaching your desired destination. Next, we will take that journey and set off toward accomplishing the goals we selected.

 Decide: Key Takeaways

- Visual representations of goals are helpful and motivating.

- Write your goals down; you will be much more likely to accomplish them!

- Think about your whole life when making your goals.

- Put your goals through the tests: are they SMART, exciting, and connect to your *why?*

- Consider that setting goals and writing them down makes them much more likely to be accomplished.

- Make sure your inner voice is a positive one! You've got this!

PHASE 3: DELIVER

Delivering Results Against Your Goals, Practicing, and Adjusting

If you like taking action, this phase will be your favorite! This is when we truly get to put our foot on the accelerator and go! The hard work of planning and deciding is complete; now it is time to deliver. Once we establish our goals, it is time to begin changing our behavior, managing our time, and prioritizing our energy around accomplishing these goals. Goals are instrumental to us, but we will inevitably feel frustrated if we do not do the work that will propel us toward accomplishing our goals. The sturdy hull of our ship was constructed with diligence and perseverance. Now, our direction and destination are clear. It's time to set sail and launch into our future.

In this phase, we move from planning to doing the work. You have your goals and action items. You will build on the excellent foundation you have set up for yourself in both this process's discovery and the decision phases. The ship is strong and ready, and the destination is clear. Now it is time to shove off and sail this ship far and wide and get our sea legs.

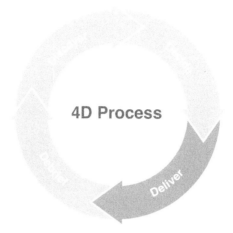

Changing Your Calendar to Accomplish Your Goals

What is the easy first step? Change your calendar! We make progress toward accomplishing our goals when we dedicate time in our calendars to focus on the work we need to do. We cannot be effective if we remain passively hopeful for change to arrive. Wishing for things is different from planning for them. If a "goal is a dream with a deadline," set the deadline on your calendar.

What would you like to accomplish this month to achieve these goals? Where will you find time on your calendar to work toward this? One of the biggest challenges in making progress is effectively scheduling. The calendar is often full, and the new priority might not have any space to land. What to do?

Get your calendar out now. Let's look ahead to the next week or 10 days. Let's implement the steps to make our goal a reality. When you change your calendar, you are making your future happen.

FIRST, BIG ROCKS

Your calendar reveals your top priorities. Consider how your schedule reflects your values. I use the term *big rocks* for these top priorities, the things you do that are directly aligned with your values. Often, our time gets chipped away with little commitments considered time fillers or even time wasters, things we do easily to delay jumping into the important things on our list. To establish progress on the big rocks, you must put them in your schedule first and then defend your ability to accomplish these tasks first. Before getting distracted by a new email notification or answering an unexpected phone call, prioritize, identify, and put the big rocks for the day into your calendar.

Now, glance over your calendar for the week ahead. Schedule time and prioritize the big rocks right now.

 REFLECT Take five minutes with your calendar. Take action based on your honest reflection.

- Is there anything you need to move to accommodate the ideas you outlined earlier?

- Block time for any "big rocks" you have for the upcoming week ahead.

- Look at what you have scheduled for this week and next. Take time to confirm or reschedule appointments or commitments.

Act now, utilize this energy, and look for all the ways to deliver.

> You may be familiar with Stephen Covey, the author of several essential books on personal effectiveness, who used the concept of "big rocks." Big rocks represent the important things in our lives. Mark Nevins writes for *Forbes Magazine*, "The origin of the "Big Rocks" concept is unknown; however, Stephen Covey popularized it in his book, *The Seven Habits of Highly Effective People.* Stories can be powerful metaphors, and once you hear this one, you may find it easier and more intuitive to keep your big rocks in the front of your mind."[15] We will use this metaphor when referring to priorities that align with your goals.

Early in my career, I attended a seminar given by Covey where he demonstrated with concept with a fishbowl, rocks, pebbles, sand, and water. At first, Covey took the empty fishbowl and displayed it for everyone. He then poured in the water, then sand, then pebbles, and when it was time to put in the "big rocks," there was little room, and the fishbowl overflowed.

When he demonstrated this a second time, he put the big rocks in first, then the pebbles, which fell into the spaces available, then the sand, which found nooks and crevices left by the big and small rocks, and finally, the water was poured into the tank. The water filled the open gaps, and the fish tank became full. You might want to watch this on YouTube to see the visuals.

Do you have your big rocks on your calendar for next week before the week is filled with sand, pebbles, and water?

WORKING ON THE RIGHT THINGS - IMPORTANCE VS. URGENCY

Another tool that Covey contributed regarding personal productivity comes with the following grid that helps us quickly evaluate and assess all of our to-do tasks. The grid relies on the two elements of urgency and importance. [16]*Consider these quadrants of time*:

Quadrant 1
Crisis
Pressing Problems
Deadline driven projects

IMPORTANT

Quadrant 2
Relationship building
Finding new opportunites
Long-term planning
Preventive activities
Personal growth
Recreation

URGENT   NOT URGENT

Quadrant 3
Interruptions
Emails, calls, meetings
Popular activities
Proximate, pressing matters

NOT IMPORTANT

Quadrant 4
Triva, busy work
Time wasters
Some calls and emails

Typically, the big rocks land in quadrant two, with things that are actionable, important, and not urgent.

How do you prioritize things as you go about your day? When you think of everything on your task list, each has a unique value. We need to consider two elements: How *important* is this task to accomplishing your future self? How *urgent* is it to accomplish?

Take out your to-do list. Look at it. Answer some of the following questions:

- How important is this task compared to other things on my to-do list this week?

- What is the urgency for completing this task?

- Will the urgency change if I do not get to this task today or this week?

- Is this task something urgent or just important?

- Are there things on my list that are *not* important?

- Is this task directly connected to accomplishing my goal?

 JOT IT Take a minute to categorize your own to-do list in the following chart.

Let's look at each item on your to-do list or calendar and categorize where the action item should fall on this chart. Consider their inherent importance and urgency.

	Urgent	Not Urgent
Important	1	2
Not Important	3	4

 JOURNAL IT Take a deeper look by considering writing in your journal here if you need more space and if this is really resonating for you.

Think about how you spend your days.

- What other areas of time do not hit upon your to-do list?

- Where would you put checking your email or scheduling a team meeting?

- Where would you put industry reading or the research you want to do?

- Where would you put activities that fall within your personal life?

- Where is Netflix or watching a game on TV?

- How about cleaning up the kitchen? Do you do the household chores in your home?

Is delegation an option? Where does laundry fit in, or how about reading to the children? Do you do the drop-offs and pick-ups? What about personal reading time or continued education and learning? Do you spend time doing the nonessential activities that fill you up? Are you a sports fan, and do you spend your Saturdays or Sundays watching games? No judgment…just nudging you to think about how you spend your time.

 CLIENT PEEK

When the CEO calls, this creates a sense of urgency. I believe this is pretty common in organizational dynamics. One client CEO had the habit of calling everyone on his team, mostly unscheduled, to get quick updates on items to evaluate progress from different anecdotal data that they collected. I was able to talk with the CEO about these "fire drill" information-gathering urgencies that they were creating. Instead of making phone calls, the CEO now takes one time a week to craft email messages to the different team members. Now, the email messages go out with a time delay option so that they are sent early Monday morning for every member of the team to open, read, and respond to. Moving this important conversation from an interrupting phone call to a timed email where team members can respond less urgently has helped the dynamics. Simply moving something from quadrant 1 to quadrant 2 can make a meaningful change. If you lead a team, think about what urgency you might be creating and if it is appropriate or if it simply is creating a fire drill for others.

Plan Ahead for the Urgent Request

While we cannot change other people's behavior, if you are always dealing with urgent requests from your manager, I suggest you try to preempt these interruptions. Schedule a predictable meeting with your boss each week to connect. If you have that time allocated, you can push the conversation to that timeframe or quickly address the urgent interruption and mention, "We can talk further at our one-on-one meeting this week." We have to defend our plans and our peak working times.

BE INTENTIONAL WITH YOUR CALENDAR

Take control of your time! We know we do not get time back, so carve out space on your calendar for activities aligned with your values. Your calendar should directly reflect your intentions. Make room for nonurgent but important tasks. Blocking time on your calendar for days and months to come helps you accomplish your goals. Do not undervalue the quadrant 2 activities, which are important and not urgent items. Relationships are built and maintained when people make time, often for conversations that are not urgent.

📇 CLIENT PEEK

Some of my clients have had specific goals for selling, either formally with a quota or a less formal goal for selling the services of their business. When I work with a client who is focused on how to be more effective with selling, a great first step is to look at their calendar. When we take a deep dive into their calendar, looking at each activity that they have scheduled, we ask, how is this meeting or activity contributing to bringing on new business? A common tendency is to stay in our comfort zone and keep busy without working on the things that truly drive results. So, it is important to look at what activities on your calendar will drive results and what activities are ancillary to that. A strategy to start today is to block time on your own calendar for goal accomplishment and dedicate a certain number of hours per week to that end.

Take notice of when you schedule your upcoming week.

- Do you take time on Sunday night to plan for your upcoming week?

- Do you plan on Friday for the following Monday?

- Do you prefer a "loose" calendar, being more spontaneous?

When we tell ourselves we are not planning too much so we can be "ready for the crisis," does this actually mean we are putting off working on the hard things?

 REFLECT Be honest with yourself and consider if you need more structure and planning in your week.

On your calendar, determine your quadrant two tasks and schedule these first. Defend tasks that are not urgent but very important against unexpected distractions. This habit becomes a crucial practice. Suppose you have time booked to work on a project tied to your values, and something comes up, for example. In that case, if your manager sends a meeting request or an urgent medical issue arises, rather than canceling your plan for your project, you can recalibrate and reschedule.

Beware of the Busyness Trap!

Know the difference between being busy and being effective. The invention of the smartphone compromised our attention and focus. The instant-gratification, get-it-right-now culture we live in represents an added pressure. We are often unaccustomed to working on projects that do not have a sense of urgency. We need to remind our brain, our conscious mind, that often, the most important things in our lives are not urgent. Spending time with family, reading, learning something new, and taking vacations are effective ingredients for future productivity. These examples illustrate the value that non-urgent yet important obligations play in our lives. Suppose we miss these recharging elements and push them off for too long. In that case, they become urgent, even critical—like a neglected relationship or a planned vacation continuously postponed.

> *Harvard Business Review* published an article in the March/April issue of 2023 entitled "Beware a Culture of Busyness." In the article, psychologist and author Adam Waytz makes the case that busyness has become a status symbol. When asked, "How are you doing," an answer is commonly "busy," as if this is the metric for success. However, activity is not a metric for success, he writes. [17]Do not get stuck into thinking that because your calendar is full of activities and events, these activities and events will result in your definition of success and accomplishing the goals you outlined earlier. Let's focus on ensuring our calendar's time slots lead to desired outcomes.

So often, we put ourselves last on our priority list. The boss, the kids, and the urgent daily issues grab our time and attention. Having a calendar with goals aligning with our values, we cannot skip carving out that time for our goals, even when the emergency hits. Do not let your hard-won planning drop off your radar. Carve out time in the future and rearrange to get your priorities on your calendar. You will be delighted with your ability to pivot effectively.

Put yourself on your priority list first and avoid the "busyness" trap. I know this is easier said than done!

CLIENT PEEK

I work with a lot of self-described workaholics who take minimal vacation days a year and may lose their vacation days altogether at the end of each year. Some clients are proud of this commitment to being at work or in their offices. I will never forget when I met a true workaholic when I was interviewing a young man while collecting feedback for one of my clients. This person took "living at the office" quite literally. This individual shared with me that he slept in his office to maximize his time at work. When I asked him about vacation, he reported that he takes virtual vacations on his computer to see other countries. I made certain that this employee knew of my concern; his strategy in the short term would lead to regret in the long term. It took a lot of discussion, but this employee is no longer sleeping at work. The dedication seems impressive, yet the cost is too great.

Now, consider what is most important and strategize more time on your calendar for the essential nonessentials.

KNOW YOUR PEAK ENERGY TIMES

Each day, we experience energy highs and lows. If you are working in a traditional office, sometimes getting things accomplished before the hustle and bustle of the day is most effective. I prompt clients to find their best "in the zone" time for work. For many, tackling a project in the morning is effective. Having a realistic deadline for lunch serves as a helpful break. For others, holding meetings or collaborating might be more effective in the afternoon when people are more awake and open to discussion. We may be most effective at varying times of the day. Some people do their best work in the evenings. One of my clients does all their important work between 4:30 a.m. and 5:30 a.m. Whatever the time, know you.

Did you ever start your day knowing that you had an important goal to accomplish, but you decided to do all the little things first—make sure your desk is well-organized and the office is clean—only to put off time to devote full attention to this critical project? It's a c common habit for many! However, when we use up our mental energy organizing our papers or making decisions about our email, by the time we get to our project, we are drained.

Decision-making takes energy! Research has found that decision fatigue can be a real challenge. Estimates suggest adults make more than 35,000 decisions in a day. [18]Each of these decisions takes brain power. Think about it: As our first decision of the day, do we kick the sheets off and hop out of bed, or do we press that snooze on our alarm and try to get a couple more minutes of sleep? Do we start early and make coffee or tea, or do we try to get some exercise first? What are we wearing today? Will we do some chores around the house or get right to work? What are we feeding the dog, our children, or ourselves? What route do we take to work? Are we stopping for gas, or can we make it a few more days on a quarter tank? Do we make calls or listen to a podcast during our commute? We might make thousands of decisions before lunchtime.

CLIENT PEEK

One client I worked with intended to start his creative work on Friday afternoons. It sounds logical as his plan was to finish his commitments for the week and then have a clear head because his weekly work commitments would be complete. I challenged him on this, and yet he insisted. So, after a few weeks, our discussions had him truly looking in the mirror. He finally capitulated that it would be best if he started his big projects earlier in the week.

We can all fall into the trap of thinking that we need to finish all of our time-sensitive work and then leave the "extra time" at the end of the day or week for pursuits that are important but not time-based. The challenge is that there is often no time left when we have already committed our clear minds and our mental energy to the first part of the week, and on Friday afternoons, we have little left in the tank.

These tasks we run through each day do not begin to cover the internal decisions we make. In each moment, we choose our mood and our outlook. Our brain has a negativity bias and automatically looks for threats. We are all running around with internal narratives as we start our days. "What else can go wrong today?" is a common mantra that may have slipped into your daily direct messages to yourself. Perhaps that statement has become your standard mode of operating.

Have you ever had such a long day that when it comes to dinner time, when someone asks, "What do you feel like for dinner tonight?" you respond with, "I don't care; fix anything; I don't want to have to make one more decision!"

Keep your energy in mind and try to block time out for when you know your energy will be high, mentally and physically, to tackle the big things. Are you ready to jump into a project and use your fresh energy, or are you trying to fill in little things to procrastinate the start? When scheduling events and blocking off time toward your goals, be brutally honest with yourself. If you pick Friday at 3 p.m. to start working on your big goal, is this your optimal time to focus more on being creative, accomplishing each task, and feeling energized for the weekend ahead, or are you fatigued after a long, hard week?

Recognizing how many decisions we make a day is surprising. I coach clients to try to streamline their calendars so they preserve their energy for the big decisions they may face. Start the day with the same routine and with one strategy to keep decision-making minimal. Know your time allocated to email and stick with that time commitment. Hold your staff meeting at a similar time each week.

> ### Strive for Less Decision-Making in Your Day
>
> I found a great illustration of minimal decision-making in an interview with the best-selling author Stephen King. He talked about how each time he worked on writing a book, he would have the same lunch every day. The lunch choice was a tuna fish sandwich for one whole book or peanut butter and jelly for another book. He never used one brain cell to decide what to eat. Instead, he would use his decision-making and creativity for the book he was writing.[19]

Each day, consider the areas in your life where you can streamline your decision-making and preserve your mental energy. Planning critical decisions before your tank is empty is helpful. Do what you planned on your calendar and use your brain energy to address the things that might arise unexpectedly.

Practicing Discipline and Focus

Now that we have aligned our calendar with our values and goals, let's prepare for accomplishment. It takes discipline and focus to work toward a goal. Putting in the reps at the gym builds muscle. Grinding through the tedious tasks accomplishes the project. Diligence in each aspect of a plan is what makes progress. Momentum creates more energy. Perhaps you get energized and revved up by accomplishing some quick tasks as a warm-up, or maybe you write "plan my day" as task 1 so you can have a quick win to check off your list once that is complete. You might finish a task and get that dopamine hit that comes with checking something off your list.

Discipline is a constant commitment to the present moment. In business and life, practice is a non-disputable way to improve performance. As humans, the experience of doing repetitive things provides our brains and bodies with data that we can either adjust or replicate. Consider how you can incorporate practice in this phase as you look to deliver against the goals that you have set.

Practice Field

In his book, *The Fifth Discipline*, Peter Senge was the first to declare that we need more practice in business. In sports and entertainment, where people perform for a living, practice is integrated into the process. The more times an NBA star stands at the free throw line and hits the shot, the more muscle memory this athlete builds to perform under every condition. Practice builds muscle memory and creates more successful outcomes. Consider how you will build in practice time.

TAKE TIME NOW TO USE YOUR TOOLS

Your tools will support building discipline. Using these tools will help you accomplish your goals. Remember, you are in the driver's seat. You are steering this ship. Each of these tools uniquely helps with goal achievement. You decide if you want to use one tool, even when prompted for another.

 REFLECT Be honest with yourself. What is easy for you, what comes naturally, and what is more of a challenge? Set up some time for your goals and try precise future planning. Science confirms the effectiveness of saying your self-talk and making your plans out loud.

BUDDY UP If you have someone else to check in with, this is a proven method to stay accountable. You might review your calendar with a colleague, spouse, or even your assistant at work. Simply "saying things out loud" and sharing them with a buddy is a powerful tool.

 JOURNAL IT Your journal can be the most helpful tool to engage with during this time for delivering against your goals. How will you keep track of your progress? Here are some prompts to get you started:

- Today, I did the following _____ to work toward accomplishing my goal of _____.

- Where do I get distracted? Roadblocks and barriers to my goal include: _____
  _____

- Working toward this goal has me thinking about these other goals: _____
  _____

- Three new ideas that will help me accomplish this goal include: _____

_____

_____

_____

Our journal is a place to save ideas for future goals. Building the practice of journaling will help us develop more discipline to accomplish our planned goals. Let's stretch a little further; soon, we will be ready to go further still. Take time to use these tools.

LEARN HOW OUR BRAIN WORKS AGAINST US

In reality, our brain works against us as we try to create the discipline we desire. We have already mentioned that our brain has a negativity bias, so we are predisposed to look for the negative. This bias sees the half-empty glass. The brain and our neurochemistry are eager to get quick results, wins, and immediate satisfaction. Our brains also feel a constant stream of interruption in our modern world. So many distractions are drawing our attention, and it is getting harder to produce the focus required to work with discipline toward goal completion. Additionally, part of our brain, the limbic system, is wired for procrastination.[20]

Let's investigate procrastination and *endorphin/dopamine* hits as this explains why starting on the big rocks feels so hard. Fortunately, we know so much more about how the brain functions than even a decade ago, so we have insight and data to help us rewire our habits and recommit to the discipline that will pay off in helping us accomplish our goals.

In his book released in 2022, *Stolen Focus*, Johann Hari provides an in-depth analysis of all the elements that steal our focus in our modern age. One of his key findings is that we are not personally responsible for our declining focus; rather, many external forces and intentional technologies are working against us. We do not need a scientific study to confirm what our own experiences reveal: our cell phones are addictive and distracting. The notifications, the access to information 24/7, and the ability for anyone anywhere to get in touch with us, if we have cell phones, all contribute to our diminishing attention span.

Hari also explains the neuroscience behind the inability to multitask effectively. We may think that our brain can focus on multiple things simultaneously, but this is a false assumption. Instead, our brains lose so much time by "switching," as he describes, from one task to another, weakening our focus.

His research coincides with interviews conducted with Professor Gloria Mark at the Department of Informatics at the University of California, Irvine. Hari published Mark's findings that "the average American worker is distracted roughly once every three minutes. Several other studies have shown that many Americans are constantly interrupted and switching between tasks. The average office worker now spends 40 percent of their work time (wrongly) believing they are 'multitasking'—which means they incur energetic costs for their waning attention and focus." [21]Uninterrupted time is becoming a rare commodity, indeed.

Distractions, the time our brain has taken on "switching" between tasks, and external and internal triggers all work against us as we pursue our goals. Be aware of your cell phone and recognize that our brains are not set up for multitasking!

TAKE CONTROL: CIRCLE OF CONTROL, CIRCLE OF INFLUENCE, CIRCLE OF CONCERN

We must consider what is inside or outside our control. There are things we *can* influence, so if we tackle those first, perhaps we will succeed more when we face the elements that are simply outside our control. A helpful way to look at this more deeply is to consider for yourself what is in your control and what is outside of your control. Simply put, there are things in your circle of control, things that are just outside of your control that you can influence, and then things that are truly out of your control—that you still may have a concern about—yet no real role in impacting directly. Use the following examples to consider what is inside your own circle of control and influence.

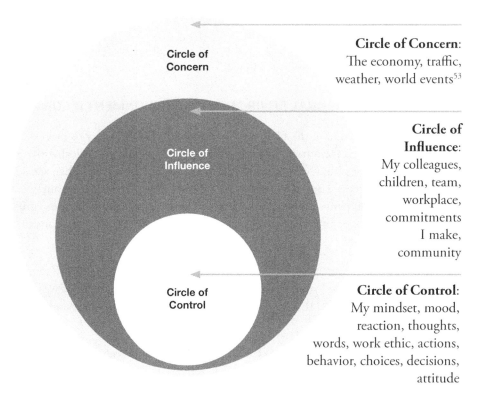

Circle of Concern: The economy, traffic, weather, world events[53]

Circle of Influence: My colleagues, children, team, workplace, commitments I make, community

Circle of Control: My mindset, mood, reaction, thoughts, words, work ethic, actions, behavior, choices, decisions, attitude

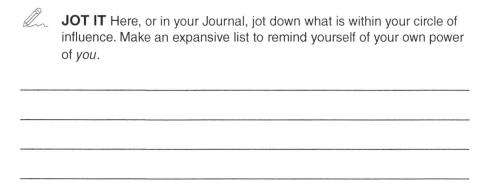

JOT IT Here, or in your Journal, jot down what is within your circle of influence. Make an expansive list to remind yourself of your own power of *you*.

_____

_____

_____

_____

Changing Your Environment

Many factors will be outside our circle of control and influence, yet we will examine some of the things we can impact.

CHANGE YOUR EXTERNAL ENVIRONMENT: ENVIRONMENT BY DESIGN

Our environment is one of the biggest factors that affects our ability to meet our goals. Too often, we take our environment for granted; we accept or deal with where we land. Assessing your environment should be an initial step when setting yourself up for success. I am not simply talking about the physical space but also what else is happening around you. Are you working in a Starbucks, in your basement, or at a cube in a busy corporate office? Consider the pros and cons of your environment.

The goal is to create the right external environment for yourself so you are much more likely to be able to create a deep, immersive focus—the same focus we introduced earlier—called the *flow state*. Consider your environment closely and look for the following:

- **Distractions**: Is there a way you can minimize the environmental elements that will draw your attention and focus? Lately, with hybrid office settings, we can work remotely from anywhere. Some settings offer more or better resources than others. Is there a window with people moving outside your workspace? Do you have distractions from food or drink? Know yourself and limit things that will take you off-track.

- **Resources**: Does your environment have everything that you need to keep moving forward toward your goal achievement? Do you need your phone handy with a charger, or are there people with whom you need to collaborate to be effective? Do you need office supplies to get organized? You know your resource needs, so make sure you have them.

- **Best energy for *you***: Do you prefer a dim or highly lit environment? Do you work well with clutter and lots of easy-to-reach supplies on your desk or with a clear desktop? Think about setting yourself up for success without falling into the trap of cleaning your desk all day instead of working toward your goals. There is a balance! If you are often cold and your office gets dark, make sure you have lighting and perhaps a blanket on hand. If you need a clutter-free workspace, clean up each night before your day starts the following day.

- **Other people**: Sometimes, we need role models. Seeing other people getting things done may help, so consider working around other productive people. A library, an office, or even a coffee shop could provide this. Remember that some coffee shops may include your neighbors or friends. Select a secret location so you do not fall into the distraction trap!

- **Space appropriate for the task**: Having a place for everything is helpful to prompt our brain to focus on the task assigned in the place we usually do it. Know yourself and create a workspace that energizes you. Sometimes, by taking my laptop to the coffee shop or even the kitchen, I get a burst of energy to continue and focus. Know yourself and be honest about this one!

- **Show up for the part**: Think about the best way to get yourself in the physical and mental state that your work demands. Are you appropriately dressed for the challenge regardless of your work environment? If you have sweatpants on and slippers, consider how this influences your attitude toward your work. Do you look like a professional if you are doing something that requires professionalism?

We all can take a minute to be honest about our environment. When my son was a first-year student in college, he moved into the only all-male dorm on campus. During orientation, he experienced many social advantages of living in this dormitory. Older students remarked this was a place with a constant party environment. The lifelong camaraderie and relationships fostered in this dorm were legendary. When my son moved in, I wanted to ensure he knew there would be pros and cons—challenges and positive aspects—to dorm life. In his first semester, my son learned that campus police responded quickly to check on shenanigans at his dorm. His environment was distraction-central, interruptions squared!

A month or two later, when my son realized he had mid-term exams ahead, he called me to inquire about coaching strategies to best prepare and focus in such a sea of distractions. His environment was not conducive to setting him up for success. How could he focus on studying for his exams when his world was (*predictably*) unpredictable? A simple change to your environment will pay off. A move to the campus library for my son was all it took. I see this with many corporate worksites. Cubes and meeting rooms are choices that many can make every day; headphones are often great options, too.

JOT IT Take a Minute to Write

What is the ideal setting for you to accomplish your goals? _____

_____

What ideas do you have about creating your best environment? _____

_____

Let Go of Limiting Beliefs: Imposter Syndrome

Just as you create the right external environment for success, you must also create an internal environment for success.

Imposter syndrome is a particular type of internal talk or labeling. We have all felt this way occasionally, but the habit of thinking you are somehow a fraud in your field is not helpful. Simply put, the feeling or belief you don't belong, you don't deserve where you are, or you don't deserve what you are doing becomes dangerous to your self-esteem. If you label yourself as an imposter, you might believe it!

Our major barrier to success is often ourselves and our unchecked thinking. Sometimes, our established mental framework influences our behavior and, therefore, the impressions others have of us. Many clients share that imposter syndrome is one of their greatest challenges. They struggle with internal questions like "Am I even qualified for this?" or "Who is going to find out I'm not ready for this task."

When you notice this demeaning internal talk, you must challenge and redirect it to create new neural pathways that lead us straight to our goal. If you have a disruptive thought of "I am not qualified to be here," the first step is to flip it to a statement of confidence: "I am qualified to be here."

 CLIENT PEEK

A client I was working with was the youngest professional on the team of leaders. While he had valid concerns, we replaced his imposter thinking with a broad range of essential information and talents vital to his thinking. I helped him see and believe he possessed valuable insights he could bring to the table where his older, more seasoned leadership team could not see what he saw from his youthful perspective. We used examples like "experience with all of the leading-edge technologies," "fresh eyes on this problem," and "a more diverse point of view to consider the decisions," which were based on his age, gender, and experience. A shift in mindset considers ways to think about all you bring forth instead of focusing on comparing yourself to others with different levels of experience and wisdom. Think about your unique abilities and remind your brain of positive messages.

JOURNAL IT

Remember, in the discovery part of this process, we started with your strengths. When you are actively working toward meeting your goals, this is an excellent time to provide yourself with some positive feedback. Take a minute to look back at your journal or the previous pages of this book and see how far you have come in this process. What thought pattern do you want to leave behind? What internal dialogue is in your way?

I find clients have voices in their heads that do not represent the positive, optimistic energy I try to bring to every relationship. The internal voice that people share is often the critic.

 CLIENT PEEK

One of my clients confided he has me on one shoulder and calls me "Angel"; on his other shoulder is his voice, "Devil." While working together, he would tap the angel, ask himself, "What would Mazie tell me right now?" and bring in more positive internal messages. Positive messages and mantras remind us of what is helpful, powerful, and effective. To be successful, you need to amplify your angelic, constructive, optimistic voice.

Internal messages you tell yourself must align with the success of accomplishing this goal and should work to your benefit, not work against you. Often, our mindset gets in the way at this point; we may use internal talk that pushes us to question why we are working on a goal. To succeed, we must counter the volley of the devil's negative thoughts with an angel who knows when to intervene with self-worth and compassion. How long does it take for you to recognize the devil's voice has taken over? Your self-talk is important here. We revisit and reinforce this skill by creating a positive internal environment, and our voice *is* that powerful. Since we are not working together and meeting frequently, I am counting on you to ensure you hear my voice, too. You've got this. You are in charge! Remember to speak to yourself with great care and awareness.

JOT IT Consider completing the following chart for yourself:

Initial Message (Devil Language)	Flip It (Angel/Coach Language)

Building Helpful Habits

One of the most powerful ways to set ourselves up for success is to create habits that align with our goals. Habits allow us to lower the volume of internal self-doubting questions and act in our best interest.

Habits help us make fewer decisions and maintain our practice toward achievement until they are no longer choices but engrained ways of being.

If we intentionally start each day focused on our big rocks consistently, this will eventually become a habit. If we create anchor habits for our work life and personal goals, we can spend less time deciding what is next and possibly risk going off track.

Habits are powerful in creating automatic behaviors. In February 2021, *Harvard Business Review* published "What Does it Really Take to Build a New Habit?" Author Kristi DePaul wrote that research shows "around half of our daily actions are driven by repetition."[22]

James Clear's research and contribution in his popular book, *Atomic Habits,* have helped us understand what makes a habit, how to establish helpful habits, and how to break habits that may be harmful in our lives.

Clear defines habits as "automatic choices that influence the conscious decisions to follow."[23] Autonomic, or automatic, behaviors that don't require conscious brain power are essential for survival. Breathing, blinking, and heartbeat are all autonomic behaviors. If you capitalize on building helpful habits, you will be more successful than if you hang on to habits and behaviors that set you back. Clear confirms *Harvard Business Review*'s findings, emphasizing that 40–50% of our daily actions are habit-based. He suggests creating more positive habits aligned with our long-term goals will make us more productive, successful, and healthier in the long run. Clear advises that stacking new habits on dependable ones allows us to have more success.

Building automaticity is the key. When things are on autopilot, we do not overthink or decide whether to continue the habit. Build your habits on a foundation of tried-and-true habits you have the proven ability to stick to.

The following "Client Peek" shares some examples of habits that I have coached my clients to establish. Consider if any of these might work for you.

 CLIENT PEEK

Sales Calls on Mondays at 3 p.m. to Set Up the Week Ahead: One client building his business was always looking for extra time to reach out to his network during the week. Thinking back to the fishbowl analogy, when you are waiting to do the important tasks and looking for time, the tasks do not often fit into your week unless you schedule them first. He hesitated to schedule things for Mondays, as the day was often busy, but after talking him through the specifics of his meetings on Monday, most activity was accomplished before the end of the day. We capitalized on a small gap of time later on Monday afternoons. Now, on Mondays at 3 p.m. each week, this leader will do reach-out calls and emails with his network. This way, he can even offer time during the week ahead for deeper connections.

Recognition Note Tuesday: One leader I worked with struggled with finding ways to recognize his staff. After we examined his calendar and identified his intention, we brainstormed, and he established a new habit. He scheduled his calendar for every Tuesday at 5 p.m., the end of his workday. He would write one personal email each Tuesday to a member of his team that demonstrated something impressive or aligned with the team's goals from the week prior. The notes were customized and personal, and they made quite an impact on his team.

Lunchtime Workout Monday and Friday: One leader I worked with had many intense goals for his professional work and was frustrated that his goals around his health were continually being thwarted or sacrificed. We talked about what he was trying to accomplish with his fitness routine, the specifics of where and what, and then we looked at his calendar for when. Based on his schedule and his proximity to his gym, he would build workouts for Mondays and Fridays at lunchtime. He found that he most often had control over these two days and could set up a specific time and place to work out and quickly return to work.

Formal Communication on the First of the Month: Another client I worked with recently was a newly appointed CEO who was establishing her reputation as a leader. We discussed her goals and created a vision for what type of leader she wanted to be known as in her company. Recognizing that, communication with her entire organization was a top priority as she sought to establish her image and build trust. Brainstorming ideas, she started with a monthly communication in person or via email on the first of each month. This predictable habit let the organization build confidence—they would know what was happening directly from the CEO every month. She quickly built upon this practice and created a valuable two-way dialogue with her workforce. No matter what your role is, having a predictable time to communicate can be quite effective.

Publishing on Friday: Some clients have significant online commitments to publish their insights. I always ask that they pick a deadline day and be predictable and consistent. Establishing a deadline, any day during the week, with a time instruction attached, prompts action.

Coffee talk Wednesday: One client leader had a large, multilevel staff working for her, and she wanted to be more available to everyone who did not directly report to her. We brainstormed, and she implemented Coffee Talk Wednesdays, where, on the first Wednesday of each month, she held virtual Coffee Talk time, where anyone in her large team could find her online to check in directly.

End-of-month wrap-up: In the spirit of consistency, buttoning things up at the end of each month, with emphasized accomplishments, is helpful. To build accountability and visibility, I have prompted many clients to establish predictable and consistent communications, whether this is an update or a status report at the end of each month. This simple step of communicating in a predictable, consistent fashion is not a common practice in many organizations and can help leaders stand out quickly.

Set yourself up for success by establishing habits that work in your favor. Spend less time thinking about what you might or could do, and simply do what your effective habits reinforce.

The following are strategies to consider:

- **See it**: A calendar on your desk with deadlines for various projects gives your brain a visual cue to prompt action toward your goals. If you have a written plan, a to-do list, or a schedule for the day ahead and hear your phone ring, you can decide whether to answer that call or let it go to voicemail. Even if you answer the phone and take care of the issue raised in the phone conversation, having a schedule for your day, with your priorities easy to see, will help you jump right back into accomplishing the task you had originally outlined. If you do not have a plan, redirecting your attention becomes more difficult after the interruption.

- **Pre-commit**: Another great strategy is to commit ahead; you need less motivation and willpower when deciding in advance. For example:

  - If you write your to-do list for work the night before, you will already be prepared to jump in on the tasks you outlined.

  - If you leave a book on your pillow, you will be more likely to pick it up to read at bedtime.

  - If you wake up and see your workout attire immediately, you are more inclined to wear your activewear and do your workout.

  - Similarly, if you wake up and have chosen a business outfit for the day, you save your decision-making energy by simply wearing a predetermined choice.

  - If you walk into your kitchen to see a bowl of fresh fruit or healthy snacks, you might eat that instead of looking for chips or chocolate.

  - If you open your refrigerator and see cut-up carrots and celery at eye level, you will likely have a healthy snack.

  - If you leave your desk at the end of each workday with the items you want to tackle the following morning, you will have less room to start with the time wasters discussed previously.

  - If you put your to-do list front and center with your agenda for the day on your desk, when you return from lunch, you will be less distracted by checking email or looking at social media.

- **Stacking habits**: Habit stacking means tying a task we would like to do to another we already do as a well-established habit. Connecting two tasks—one automatic and one desired—increases the probability of doing the new task. You can head to lunch, for example, after reading a certain number of pages or completing a certain number of tasks. The evidence is easy to recognize; the more you stack habits, the more changes you will see. Earlier, we talked about scheduling time for goal achievement in your calendar. Are there things you automatically do to which you can tie a new task? For example, if you want to write daily and you have a habit of enjoying your morning coffee in silence, can you connect writing with your morning coffee? A dedicated morning ritual that includes an already well-established activity—like enjoying a cup of coffee—will inspire deadline completion like nothing else.

  You might also consider rewarding the new behavior right away. If you make the two sales calls and then break for lunch, you can treat yourself to something tasty to reinforce and celebrate your consistency with establishing this behavior. If we need to get in more reps, look for places in your day and your week where you can insert the important but not urgent elements that contribute to you accomplishing your goals. You earn an hour listening to a podcast you enjoy after you draft your article for LinkedIn. You go outside to get fresh air and take a brief walk to enjoy the outdoors after completing your agenda for your next marketing meeting.

✎ **JOT IT** Think about your day tomorrow and capture some ideas:

- What do I want to establish as a new and improved habit? _____

_____

- How can I connect a new habit to something I already do? _____

_____

- What is the best time of day, and where will I practice this new habit? _____

_____

Getting Out of Your Own Way

Even with the smartest goals and the best habits, we will get off track, interrupted, or stuck. We can get off track from external forces or even internal thoughts. Perpetual interruptions are one of the biggest challenges we face, even when we have a great plan or an agenda for our day or week.

> Hari shares research on studying interruptions in his book *Stolen Focus*. "One study found that most of us working in offices never get a whole hour uninterrupted on a normal day…. This is happening at every level of business…even a CEO gets less than one hour daily of uninterrupted time."[24] We must be diligent about managing these interruptions.

We will review some obvious strategies here and consider brainstorming for yourself what might work best for you.

FIGURE OUT WHAT IS INTERRUPTING YOU

Perhaps your phone distracts you so much that you have become conditioned to look for the notifications each time they signal you. You might have a roommate, child, or colleague at your office who is your main source of interruption.

REFLECT Take an honest look in the mirror and identify the biggest causes of diverting your attention and veering off track. Be honest with yourself and talk out loud or jot down the truth of distraction in the pages of your journal or jot it here.

 JOT IT What are my biggest sources of interruption?

STRATEGIES TO AVOID INTERRUPTIONS

Interruptions are a part of our modern lives. While the best case would be to minimize interruptions when working toward your goals, here are a few strategies for dealing with interruptions as they arise.

Keep an Agenda for Yourself

Have an agenda for the day and outline a plan for an expected distraction rather than flounder after an interruption to figure out where you have left off. If you have timeframes for activities throughout the day, you can decide where to compensate for the time spent with the distraction. You can jump right back on course if you have a plan to start with each day.

> In further studies in *Stolen Focus*, Hari researchers monitored school students for how long it took them to return to focus after an interruption. On average, it took 23 minutes to return to the level of focus the student experienced before the interruption. Knowing where you left off can help.[25]

Set Expectations for Yourself and Others

Another tool to implement is to set expectations for yourself or others for the duration you are willing to give to the interruption.

Let's face it, our brains avoid doing hard things. Concentrating is hard, especially with our technology tools contending with our shortened attention spans. With all the cell phone applications, games, and communication platforms, one could spend most of their time looking at their phone screen.

Recognize that we are in the driver's seat and must reclaim our time with intent and healthy technology habits—not just for optimal brain function and performance but to enhance our already commodified, precious time and energy. Setting clear expectations will create healthy boundaries for answering your email or picking up your phone. Consider setting consistent times of day to check your phone or email. You can already predict that messages will pull your attention from your original plan for your day. Timestamp with a notation on your agenda or calendar or set the alarm on a watch or phone timer.

Be honest. Look back at what is important/urgent/not important/not urgent and be transparent with where most of the time these distractions fall. Keep devices possibly in another room when you need to be sharp and mindfully on task when needed.

Dealing with interruptions can be most challenging as we are not in control of other people. The following are some strategies that I have offered my clients.

 CLIENT PEEK

Set expectations from the start: If you are working on a project and your phone rings or someone pops by your office, consider starting the conversation with a warm greeting and then setting the expectation quickly. "I'm glad you called, as I look forward to connecting with you. Right now, I only have 10 minutes to talk. Can we jump in and carve out more time later this week to discuss this topic further?"

Give cues: If a person stops by your office, it is helpful to stand as they enter. Your action gives a visual cue to the person that you are heading out or moving on to another task. You can also use this language: "I'm glad you caught me; I only have five minutes to connect. If we need more time, let's circle back this week."

Walk people back to their desks: Often, our nonverbal cues are enough to manage an in-person interruption. This tactic works great if you are in an office setting. If we greet someone, cover a topic, and walk them back to their office or cubicle, they will most likely re-engage with their work once they arrive. I am always amazed by this subtle nudge's effectiveness; we need not utter a word in the process.

Schedule a 23-minute meeting: Another helpful idea is to block time that is less than the default hour. I have had clients report success when implementing strategies for 23-minute meetings or "huddles." If you consider a 40-minute team discussion, perhaps you will all benefit from the balance of the 20 minutes of unscheduled time.

Meetings, meetings, and more meetings: Most successful clients have "meetings with themselves" on their calendars. We must face the reality that our workday can sometimes be one nonstop back-to-back day of meetings. So, how do we remain effective and productive when we sit in meetings all day? The best strategy is to block time for ourselves. Take a look at the calendar right now. Do you have enough time within the next week to prepare for meetings or follow up on meetings? Are there priorities you need to accomplish that you simply do at home nightly or before others get to work? If this is the case, take your calendar out and look where you see a little daylight. If you are unscheduled during certain timeframes, take the time slot for yourself and make your mental and physical health part of your agenda.

Are We Our Biggest Distraction?

While interruptions from others are frustrating, the distractions we provide ourselves present an even bigger challenge. Procrastination, distractions, overthinking, and even trying to hold ourselves back from impulsive behavior are all common challenges to tackle as we work toward our goals. Here are some ideas for each of these. Think about what's important in how you tackle a project. Is your cell phone on your desk when you work on a project? Are notifications on? Might you be addicted to taking a little "mental break" and checking email or social media?

In Blake Thorne's blog entitled "I Done This," Thorne tackles the topic of distraction. He references Gloria Mark's research at the University of California, Irvine, and takes her statistics further to investigate the impact of distracting ourselves. Thorne reveals key findings from the study: "About half the interruptions were self-inflicted. The average person in their study checked their email 74 times a day, with some people on the high end of the spectrum checking up to 435 a day!"[26] We may be our own worst distractors.

Switching, the term used to describe our shift in focus, is described by Thorne as "essentially, playing tennis with our mental energies, volleying them back and forth at a moment's notice. Only unlike a tennis ball, our brain takes a little time to switch directions." While this habit seems harmless, it takes a lot to get us back on track where we left off.[27]

FIGURE OUT WHY YOU ARE PROCRASTINATING

We usually enjoy doing things we feel confident about and activities that increase our energy. Expecting low energy and frustration associated with completing the not-so-fun tasks becomes an excellent reason to put things off just a little longer.

When we challenge procrastination and stop to consider why we put things off, we may find the answers that influence our behavior. We all may experience procrastination.

> Adam Grant, Wharton's top-rated professor, researcher, and best-selling author, provides some insight regarding procrastination in his 2022 book, *Think Again*. Grant challenges many inaccurate beliefs and assumptions and writes, "Procrastination isn't laziness. You don't put off tasks to avoid work. You do it to avoid unpleasant emotions- self-doubt, boredom, confusion, frustration." Grant further suggests that "the task you're avoiding isn't always the one you hate. Sometimes, it's the one you fear. The one that's most worth pursuing."[28]

It is important to investigate the root cause of your procrastination. We are often trying to avoid something. Are you trying to avoid boredom? Are you avoiding fear? Typically, you are avoiding a feeling. Only you can answer this question. Get curious about discovering the *why* behind your moment of procrastination. Is there a pattern?

If you are challenged with procrastination regularly, consider using your tools and trying these strategies. Let's face the root cause of procrastination.

 REFLECT Ask yourself, what is the root cause of this behavior?

 JOURNAL IT Take some time to write out your emotions about what you are procrastinating. What is the predictable result of not getting to this task? What will happen if you finish the task?

 BUDDY UP This is a great time to work with a buddy. If you have someone holding you accountable for milestones in reaching your goal, you are less likely to procrastinate. You have a relationship to uphold with your buddy. Allow them to help you overcome the delay and get to the task.

STRATEGIES TO STOP PROCRASTINATING

We can tackle our tendency for procrastination with some strategies. Creating a sense of urgency, real or fabricated, can really help. Try the following detailed strategies as you need them.

Just start—commit to two minutes: Rather than thinking about the whole project or task, nudge yourself to initiate an actionable step for two minutes. Studies have shown that making this minimum commitment to get started allows us to engage. Once we get started, we often engage in much longer periods, committed to accomplishing our goals. Say to yourself you will work on something for two minutes, which will help you get over the sometimes-illusive energy required to begin. A blank page is less scary than a page with a few sentences at the top.

Anticipate the feeling of accomplishment: Remember the feeling of accomplishing something, like the feeling at the end of a workout coming home from the gym—or that satisfying feeling when you complete a weeks-long work project? Put yourself into a physical accomplishment mindset and consider how your physiology changes when you accomplish a long-term goal. Imagine the feeling of gratification and satisfaction, as if your accomplishment is happening now. Allow that feeling to help influence and motivate you to do the task you have put off.

Work backward: What needs your attention today? This week? This month? Break down bigger projects into smaller chunks and set aggressive deadlines. Use your calendar. Put the deadlines on it now to create a sense of urgency for what needs to happen today.

Positive self-talk: Quiet the voice that says "This is so much work, or I wish I had started this earlier." Rather, flip the script and say, "I'm so glad I'm starting this now, before the deadline, so I have plenty of time to accomplish this goal." Flip the narrative to the positive and reinforce this with your brain's ability to jump-start into effective time management.

JOT IT What strategies will you use to overcome procrastination?

_____

_____

_____

STRATEGIES TO STOP UNHELPFUL BEHAVIORS: CROWDING OUT AND REPLACING

My coaching approach heavily depends on taking action. Coaching is fundamentally based on behavior change. To experience a change, we see a new behavior, experience something different, and notice a shift. Clients are frustrated when the most helpful change is to temporarily "stop doing" something as it is easier to notice when people start doing something as compared to when people stop an unhelpful behavior. It is hard to notice when we stop doing something. For example, when clients work on developing their executive presence, a lot of this work involves the difficult skill of stopping old habits that get in the way of growth. More examples include stopping interrupting, saying inappropriate or less-than-professional things in meetings, and demonstrating anger with other leaders. However, I find people are more motivated by the behaviors they can start doing right now, like taking action and making a different impression.

We can alter our thinking regarding our work behaviors, relationships, and habits. Rather than focus on words we cannot say or behaviors we are trying not to exhibit in meetings, crowd out all the possibilities and the range of things available that would be helpful to say or do. Instead of taking the approach of the absence of action, turn this practice into actions and words spoken that are more aligned with your goals.

 CLIENT PEEK

A client once came to me because the leadership team was upset with the language they used in meetings. They tended to drop the F-bomb in a conservative environment. Rather than focus on simply not saying the F-word and reminding the client repeatedly during their self-talk, "Don't say it; don't say the F-word!" we replaced the verboten expression with another word altogether. Initially, they substituted the word "flipping" just in case the "F" sound escaped too quickly. Eventually, they had fun with this and began replacing the "F" word with all sorts of fun words. Everyone noticed. Focusing on not doing something is harder than replacing that behavior with something else.

Anger or emotional outbursts are often reasons leaders seek help changing their behavior. Rather than focusing on "not yelling" when angry, a replacement habit like "taking a walk" or "breathing for a count of five" is something leaders can try. Think of a behavior or habit to replace an unhelpful habit. Set yourself up for success and focus on what you can say and what you can do, and you will be successful!

Establishing Measures To See Your Progress

Before we finish this phase—Deliver, the just-do-it phase—let's take a minute to think about how we measure progress. Measuring progress can be difficult. For this reason, it is helpful to establish some "leading indicators" to gauge early signs you are on the right track. Because we tested our goal against the SMART criteria, measurement is part of our goal. Consequently, we should be able to design, track, and measure our progress.

LOOK BACK OR LOOK AHEAD

Are you the type of person who checks their work in the middle of a project to see how much you have accomplished, or do you look at how much more you have to go? When reading a book, for example, do you look at what page number you have read up to already, or do you look at the final page of the book and subtract to see how many pages you have ahead to read? These two ways of measuring things can be called *lagging indicators* or *leading indicators*.

When discussing behavior change or goal accomplishment, we often have easy-to-see lagging indicators. Being on time for more meetings or having less email in your inbox are all indicators of productivity and time management. In our personal lives, if we change our behavior around healthy eating and are consistent, we begin to see the signs of measurable and improved health. Lower blood pressure, evidence on the scale, fewer nights snoring, more energy for fitness routines—these are all possible metrics we can look at to see if our behaviors are creating desired outcomes. Maybe our pants simply fit better, and that gives us some data that things are going well.

A challenging aspect of making behavioral change is when we have veiled or hard-to-see immediate results. We can't see amazing employee survey results the day after we start our recognition habit or an immediate productivity gain when we start planning our day. Seeing no progress, we often abandon our commitment to some goals we identified and committed to enthusiastically.

In this case, it is helpful to identify some "going forward" or leading indicators of progress. Let's identify some leading indicators. Even if we must be creative in fabricating these signs for now, we can look at measurable inputs, not just the consequences of our actions. In the previous health example, opening your refrigerator to see cut veggies and healthy proteins is a change that you can see looking ahead, and ideally, you will enjoy those foods instead of the chips that may have drawn your attention. If your goal is to get a new client, the leading indicator is to measure how many conversations you reach each week with potential clients. Changes will follow if we put the work in and do the reps. Find ways to note progress in the middle of your goal-achieving efforts.

FIND WAYS TO VISUALIZE YOUR PROGRESS

Even when our progress toward our goals is still invisible, find ways to make them easier to see. In the previous decision phase section, we covered visual ways to look at goals, which included creating a vision board. We also discussed a calendar as an easy tool to track progress.

 Take some time now to look at the visual tools to use and consider how you can measure your progress. Perhaps you look at your vision board or calendar and consider which elements you have accomplished each month. Write the names of the potential clients you have reached out to in this past month or how many clients you are actively billing each month. Visualizing progress is a crucial element that allows you to see progress to keep yourself motivated, so even when you can't easily see progress, you can find a way to measure your effort.

ADD IN METRICS FOR THE MIDDLE

When you become more familiar with your goal, you can add incremental metrics. For example, suppose you are a new manager or leader and you want to establish some practices for how often you meet with your team. Simply scheduling meetings with your team members shows a measurable activity that is aligned with your goal. If you consistently meet with your team when scheduled, without fail, this, too, becomes a metric. If you are working on a project that does not involve a team, how often do you commit to time for that project? Can you look at the tasks you have completed to show that you are making progress on the project? Even though these activities are not the end result just yet, they reflect the discipline we discussed earlier and show progress toward our goals.

CLIENT PEEK

Financial metrics are some of the easiest measures to watch. One of my clients was a sales leader, and his ultimate metric to watch was financial: how much his team sold each month. We brainstormed for leading indicators as he was re-building his sales team with new talent. Before he had financial indicators to show how much was sold each month, he was able to track the time and effort invested in this new group, which would eventually pay off. We started to measure training hours, certifications, and the number of days mentoring or teaching others. We also tracked retention and the number of days that an open role in the sales team took to fill. Looking at some nonconventional metrics and incorporating leading indicators helped us get a better picture of forecasting performance before the financial indicators came through for us to measure.

Discipline and consistency produce results if we focus on the evidence of what we've implemented and how we have changed. Hard work pays off, so find ways to measure your progress and bask in the metrics of your hard work.

 JOT IT Before we finish this phase, capture any ideas popping up and engage your mental energy. Grab your journal or get your pen and write your thoughts here.

Deliver Highlights

In this section, we looked for actions to take to deliver results on our goals. We examined ways to remove barriers and considered ways to make progress a bit easier. We have prioritized things on our calendars and, ideally, have completed some accomplishments. While on this journey, seeing direct or instant progress takes time. Our destination may still be off in the distance, beyond the horizon, and we need to keep faith in our abilities and stay the course. Establishing ways to see progress as we go is helpful; it will keep you motivated and energized.

Deliver: Key Takeaways

- Make time for your goals; change your calendar right now.

- Put your big priorities in your calendar *first*, or they will not fit.

- Differentiate between what is urgent and what is important. These are two separate things.

- Beware of the busyness trap; being busy does not mean you are working on important things.

- Decision-making takes energy; make big decisions early before you run out of steam.

- You are in control! Recognize your circle of control and circle of influence on everything, including distractions.

- Distractions are real and can derail progress. Consider how you manage them.

- Practice strategies for managing interruptions and restoring focus.

- Procrastination and trying to "not do" something are true challenges. Pick one or two new strategies to try to combat unconscious habits:

  - **Environment**: Change your scenery to increase productivity and focus more effectively.

  - **Self-talk**: Be your biggest cheerleader and focus on positive internal messages.

  - **Imposter syndrome**: Flip your thinking! Bring a unique perspective to internal dialogues.

  - **Habits**: Establish new habits to old habits you have already established. Create visual cues, pre-commit, and stack your habits for greater effectiveness.

  - **Establish Measures**: Check your vision board and find leading indicators—ways to gauge when you are in the middle.

PHASE 4: DEBRIEF
Assessing Where We Are Now and What's Next

Once you have reached this point in the process, we will arrive at our first destination on one (or several) goals we have outlined. Now, it is time to reflect, regroup, and visualize what is coming next. We are looking in the rear-view mirror now, but only to better tackle whatever is next on the journey ahead.

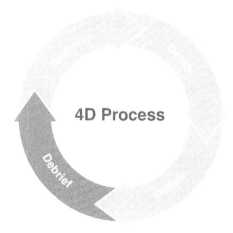

Consider this time as the sail-back-to-port leg, where you have the luxury of calm waters allowing for reflection upon the journey you have already charted. What went well, and what might you change for the next journey? What tools were helpful, and which did you earnestly avoid during this initial voyage?

First, we will look at what you accomplished, what you achieved, and your progress. Then, we will examine the learning component, what you experienced, the emotions, and the new awareness this journey provided. We take a deeper dive into looking at our mindset, examining conflict, looking at emotions, and anticipating the unexpected.

During this part of the process, it is helpful to review our experiences. The Debrief phase is a time when we can learn the most. Do not discount this section! This part of the process is the time of learning and preparing for what comes next. Reflecting on our journey will help our brain process and integrate our experiences while informing our future endeavors. This is the section where we capture wisdom!

Recognizing Accomplishments

Before we go further, we must acknowledge your achievements. Reading to this page and jotting down ideas along the way is an accomplishment in itself! You have invested the energy required to make positive changes. You are moving forward and have responded fully to the prompt "Accelerate Your Success: Let's Go!" You have a greater awareness of yourself and new ideas to try. I recognize you in the here and now and all the effort you've invested in getting this far. Transformation requires evolution, effort, sustained energy, performance, and action. Taking all the steps to accomplish your goals is worth recognizing.

 REFLECT Take a moment to return to the mirror and acknowledge yourself for every moment that has led you here.

It is so important that you recognize your progress yourself. Unfortunately, your boss or colleague may not take the time to acknowledge the good job you are doing. In Sam Jenniges' book *Recognition Rebooted*, she shares bleak statistics. She writes, "65% of North American employees report that their work wasn't recognized a single time during the prior year." Jenniges defines recognition as "taking notice of valuable impact and communicating to a team member."[29] Thus, we need to become our best allies, using self-talk to congratulate ourselves when merited.

As a reminder, words have power, especially the words we tell ourselves. When delivered meaningfully, words can serve us well, energize us, and fuel our pursuit of creating the future we want. Since I am not sitting directly across from you today to acknowledge your recent wins and accomplishments, I ask you to consider your hard work and how you have initiated and implemented change.

In addition, when our good work yields great results, our brain releases endorphins and dopamine, and this reward circuitry encourages us to replicate the feeling for future projects. Therefore, these verbalized accolades and brain-centered (biological) rewards help lead to more success.

Well done for reading and following these suggestions. Up to this point, I applaud you for taking pen to paper, for your journal entries, and for your deep work. Well done for the jot-its and the times you scheduled to meet with a buddy. Now, you can take time to reward yourself. Every action that elicits a reward is an action we like to repeat!

We, humans, like to move toward gain and away from pain. Our brains are wired that way. Consider the response or worthwhile reward for the work you have accomplished. How will you acknowledge this goal completion? If you haven't made it to your destination yet and haven't finished your goal, what redirection do you need so you will be successful with your next attempt? What pain have you experienced that will help you move forward with enhanced motivation and accomplish this goal?

 JOURNAL IT Consider your next journal entry. What will you capture from this experience of deliberately working for your goal? Without punitive measures, how will you hold yourself to account? Be creative.

If you have accomplished your goal, is there a rewarding activity or an object that can signify your achievement? How do you acknowledge *yourself* and your progress and properly reward yourself? Remember to align with the behaviors you want to continue or the person you are becoming. We want to reinforce positive behavioral changes with more of the same. Is there a professional tool that you'd like to invest in like a planner? Do you want to add something inspiring to your wall in your work environment? Is there an event you would like to attend? An upcoming professional conference that would reinforce the advances you just made? Are you interested in getting a new briefcase, bag, or portfolio? Is there something for your office you would like to invest in that will remind you of your progress? The goal's accomplishment may be a just reward, and recognizing your progress could be enough. Well done! Let's keep up our momentum and build on our accumulated progress.

CLIENT PEEK

Recently, I had a client call me to share a fantastic accomplishment. Whenever clients reconnect and share their developments, I am delighted to revel in their good news. I never take a relationship for granted, and I hope the connections I share with clients will continue for years. This client shared that they had set a goal early in his career to be acknowledged as the leader in their field by a worldwide association and finally accomplished this milestone. They called me to share the news because I was one of the only people who had a front-row seat to all of their hard work, and I could fully appreciate the depth of effort it took to accomplish this goal. When we hit a milestone, we must pause, take note, acknowledge its significance, and celebrate small and large victories.

TAKE INVENTORY

We need simple and practical tools to stay on our path to our own version of success. As you look forward to future planning, take a minute to fill out a Start-Stop-Continue list like the following one. At this stage of our work together, what actions or behaviors do you want to start doing, stop doing, or continue doing? The whole point of this is to take your own learning into account and feed it into your discovery for your next goal or action.

Start Doing	Stop Doing	Continue Doing

LEARN FROM OUR OWN EXPERIENCES

Experiential learning is easier to internalize and is often one of our best teachers. So, think about your experiences and realize which instances changed your path to accomplishment.

CLIENT PEEK

If you do not have a great role model to learn from, you can actually learn from examining your own experiences. Learning from ourselves is often more powerful than learning from others! Recently, I began working with a client who was close to retirement when we had our initial meeting, so I was eager to hear about his life experiences and how he had learned during his career. In one of our conversations, I asked if he had examples of great leaders he had looked up to as role models in his career. I was quite surprised when he shared that the only notable thing that he had learned from his direct manager was feedback to "not to start an email with the word "I." Wait, what? *Was this his key takeaway*? Like this client, you may have had poor professional role models along the way. If you haven't had a great leader, you can still learn from *yourself* by reflecting on your own experiences and determining what future actions will require adjustment.

Self-Assessing

Let's review the gap—the space between where we started and where we are now. You have new awareness and possibly new energy to tackle the next set of goals. You have momentum, forward movement, progress, and accomplishments.

Your Presenting Problem: Herein lies why you originally picked up this book. Do you still consider the presenting need to be a top priority? Or did you expand your target with our work on values, success, and the other questions you have asked yourself throughout our work together?

 JOT IT Look back at your vision board. Look back at your goal. What did you accomplish? Questions for reflection: Jot the answers here or use your journal:

- What went well? _____

- What helped you show up differently? _____

- What were the areas of struggle? _____

- Have you avoided things during this process? What? _____

- Why did you avoid them (consciously or unconsciously)? _____

Rather than reading through these questions and moving on, take a minute to really think about it and talk with a buddy.

BUDDY UP Talk with your buddy or someone you trust about your experience with this process. Articulate your experience out loud.

EVALUATE WHAT ENERGIZED OR DRAINED YOU

Reflecting on what you have accomplished thus far, it becomes helpful to consider when you were operating at your best or when you experienced the most challenge. We learn the most about ourselves when working diligently to accomplish a goal.

✐ JOT IT

• When were you at your best? _____

• When were you drained? _____

At this point, consider how you made things easier, not harder. The laws of physics give us the *principle of least action,* and we know that most of us do what is easiest, not hardest. So, how do we change our identity to align with the person we want to be?

What did you do that made achieving your goal incrementally easier for you? Did you change your schedule each day or start with the big rocks? Did you tie something you wanted to do to something you already do?

✐ JOT IT Capture your best strategies here so you have your top practices outlined for your next challenge or goal ahead:

_____

_____

_____

EVALUATE WHEN YOU WERE IN YOUR FLOW STATE

As discussed earlier, when you are so fully absorbed in something fulfilling, you cross over into a state of single-pointed focus—this is *flow.* Think back to your experience, focusing on the goal and all the actions you outlined. Was there a time that you became aware of a flow state, where time passed, and you were fully concentrating, fully absorbed, and able to perform your task(s) with greater ease? Consider this question as you think about setting future goals.

Often, we think of physical challenges that may induce a flow state akin to activities that produce an adrenaline rush—rock climbing or jumping out of a plane. However, we can also achieve flow states when immersing ourselves in self-improvement; learning about subjects that fully engage our attention can also create flow states.

Delving into Mindset, EQ, and Conflicts

By this point in our process, we recognize our power and what is in our circle of control, and everything starts with a mindset. We can choose our mindset and beliefs and encourage ourselves to grow past our limiting beliefs about ourselves and others. Our mindset is such a powerful thing! If we own our mindset, we truly can make anything happen. From the start of our journey together, your mindset of growth and improvement has been essential. At this point in the process, it is helpful to give credit to what enables our continuous learning and the confidence to achieve our future goals, and we will dive into mindset and emotions as a great place to investigate further.

> The foremost authority on mindset is Carol Dweck. Her research from Columbia University and Stanford University and her book, *Mindset*, reveal the basic belief that our mindset is not fixed; how we see things can change. She shares that activating a growth mindset is based on the internal messages we tell ourselves and that our beliefs are the key to increased states of happiness. This concept is simple yet profound.

Enthusiasm, motivation, and mindset are all defined by our emotions. So, check in with your emotions to see where you have excitement, experience joy, and what activities, thoughts, beliefs, and practices continue to bring you happiness. You are the best observer of you! Until now, our primary focus has been on taking action, getting moving, and taking initiative. Now is a time to really examine how our mental framework supports our future success.

EMOTIONS IN THE WORKPLACE

One way to measure our progress is to look at how we feel about our work lives in the new context of our total lives. Looking at the whole pie, the big picture is that we can now examine the differences between "doing" and "feeling." Let's focus on your emotional imprints and any learning you may have experienced. In addition to the goals that you achieved, you also learn from these new experiences. New awareness, beliefs, feelings, and experiences prompt us to create new neural networks. You have grown by inviting insight throughout this process; now, let's take a deeper look.

Emotional intelligence (EQ) is widely accepted as a measure of how skilled we are in knowing ourselves and relating to others.

> Daniel Goleman defines *emotional intelligence* as "the ability to recognize and regulate emotions in ourselves and others."[30] In 1995, Goldman wrote *Emotional Intelligence, Why it Can Matter More than IQ.* Shockingly, until this book came out, emotions were never topics of focus or discussed openly in the workplace. Corporate structures focused more on operational excellence, efficiency, and competency. This book and others to follow share a theory explaining why some leaders create more effective teams, why some staff and employees are more engaged and satisfied, and why companies retain talent in competitive times based on the emotional intelligence of their leaders.

Emotional intelligence consists of four competencies, which are pretty self-explanatory. [31] It is helpful to look at improving one component at a time based on the area of greatest opportunity.

It is evident from our work together that self-awareness and self-regulation are areas we have focused on for your journey toward achieving your goals.

Emotional Intelligence Competencies

Self-awareness: Your ability to have an accurate picture of yourself, your strengths, and your blind spots, as well as know your typical reactions to situations.

Self-regulation: The ability to manage yourself and know your tendencies in the moment. Knowing you might get angry with a situation and managing your emotions so as not to get as heated outwardly are examples of self-regulation.

Empathy/social awareness: Your ability to read others' emotions accurately in the moment.

Relationship management: Your ability to use your awareness of others to interact with others, build relationships, and manage conflicts with others at the moment.

Knowing yourself, your style, your strengths, and your reactions is essential for personal success. Regulating our natural tendencies to achieve the outcomes we want is also essential. We have spent less time on social awareness and relationship management, yet we certainly have included the impacts of our behaviors on others. Understanding our emotional intelligence and creating positive interactions in the workplace is now the basic expectation for all leaders. Shockingly, until the 1990s, when Goldman introduced his research on emotional intelligence, someone's emotions were not even considered as part of a person's professional success. He asserted that EQ was as important as IQ in determining our effectiveness in the workplace or other pursuits. Until this time, emotional displays were frowned upon in the workplace. Professional or not, we are emotional beings, and there are some great benefits to bringing emotions to the workplace. As a prime example, empathy would help many corporate cultures and leaders be more effective.

In my experience with clients, reviewing the leading tools on EQ is helpful and a quick study. Once someone builds self-awareness, for example, it is easy to take on new behaviors to demonstrate greater competence in any area. If more people committed to working on their EQ in the workplace, brought empathy for others, practiced self-regulation for themselves, and limited impulsive comments, workplace cultures would be more hospitable for everyone.

CONFLICT EXPLAINED THROUGH EMOTIONAL INTELLIGENCE COMPONENTS

Emotional intelligence shows us that we first start with our awareness, and then we can self-regulate and build empathy—the key factor in building strong relationships. We are responsible for our own emotions and their impact on others. If we intend to be helpful but our emotions create a high-intensity situation, or if our style makes someone else uncomfortable, we are still responsible for aligning our intentions with the outcomes we achieve.

Often, leaders may have a challenge when they struggle with self-regulation. Losing one's temper or having an "anger problem" is often used to describe someone who finds emotional self-regulation challenging to maintain. Recognizing new behavior that aligns with positive change is helpful in actuating self-regulation.

 REFLECT This is a great time to look in the mirror and predict where you are strong and where you might need to pay more attention.

- Do you believe that you have high self-awareness?

- Or are you often surprised by people's reactions to your behavior?

- Can you predict how others might receive critical feedback that you plan to give them?

Self-assess here and predict how well you do with each aspect of emotional intelligence.

> Do you want to know your measure of emotional intelligence? Travis Bradberry and Jean Greaves wrote *Emotional Intelligence 2.0,* which includes an assessment test. They recommend taking the assessment to start the process, even before reading the book, so that you know your starting point. Once you read the book and practice the new behaviors, you can retake the assessment test to see how you have improved your emotional intelligence. You will get customized scores on all four elements of EQ.

Emotional intelligence gives us a greater understanding of handling conflict. Many of my clients' *presenting* needs are related to a conflict in their workplace that they have been unable to sort out or improve. Conflict is often an unwanted addition to a relationship when emotions run high. How do we effectively manage ourselves when communication breaks down?

Emotional intelligence provides us with tools for a better understanding of a conflict between two individuals. To pinpoint the origin of a conflict, we can also look back at our preferences, which vary widely among people of different experiences and backgrounds. If a colleague has different priorities from what we believe to be most important, then conflicts are to be expected. Most often, a style mismatch is a reason conflict arises in the first place. One person might focus on a task and neglect to tend to a relationship, or someone else might go too slowly or quickly for the other person. No matter the cause of conflict, we can work things out if everyone is willing to engage.

Tackling Conflict

I realize facing conflict with integrity can be an "easier said than done" situation. However, I have never seen a conflict simply disappear if left unresolved. State clear and concise intentions, acknowledge mistakes, and use equitable and emotionally intelligent language; relationships will continue to grow and strengthen.

More often than not, conflict is a reason that a leader might engage with a coach. Regardless of a conflict's origin, I always recommend addressing the conflict directly and as quickly as possible. Unless the conflict resolves itself or the parties discontinue working together, getting ahead of a conflict is urgent before more damage occurs. We never want to ignore the elephant in the room and hope it goes away. Rather, we address the issues, call them out, and diffuse their power before further escalation.

Here are some ideas that I share with clients regarding conflict:

Take ownership of your role in the conflict.

Even if things were someone else's fault, there are often two people who have contributed to the conflict.

Share your intention up front, quickly and in earnest.

I have clients share the word *intention* directly, as it clarifies things. "I intended to be helpful. That is why I took on the project. I did not anticipate my actions would impact you in this way."

Change your language.

Change your language. Language goes a long way! Here are some examples of making subtle changes that can significantly impact outcomes:

"I disagree."	vs.	"Let's consider this from another perspective."
"I can't."	vs.	"I will; I just need to find the right time."
"You are wrong."	vs.	"Help me understand your point of view."

Invest in the relationship moving forward.

Even if you remember the difficult feelings of a conflict, try to work past them and continue building the relationship. When we get to know people beyond a task or a project, we can develop common ground or mutually beneficial goals. Sometimes, I'll have people share a statement like, "I know we both want what is best for the company, so in the future, I will take extra time to listen to be sure I'm on the same path as you." Find areas of commonality and set united goals.

I have seen the best outcomes originate from conflict. When leaders face adversity, an opportunity to invest in repairing a relationship and making it stronger arises. Leaders who openly accept responsibility for things that go wrong build trust.

🔍 CLIENT PEEK

I was working with a CFO of a large international company, focusing on strategies and habits for building accountability within his team and how powerful it is to take ownership when we make mistakes. People learn more from correcting mistakes than from perfect performance. In the third month of our coaching relationship, an error was made by one of the finance team members and received attention worldwide. This CFO released, in writing, what had happened and took full responsibility for the error. I was so proud and inspired by this action, as this honest move relieved their staff. The international leaders acknowledged that everyone makes mistakes and allowed the company to amend the error quickly.

Address the conflict directly and take ownership; it pays off.

UPCOMING GOALS

The beauty is that this process is cyclical! Every ending is a new beginning. Like life, we can continue to learn, grow, and progress toward the professional we want to become. How do you keep moving? Discover, decide, deliver, debrief, and repeat!

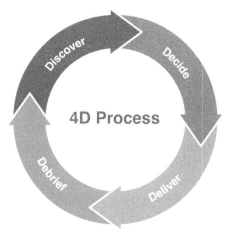

Here is your chance to recalibrate for future success. Take a minute to reflect on your identity. What or who is prompting you to set your next goal? Perhaps you want to expand your influence or create a legacy for which you want to be known. Let your future identity inspire you. When you look in the mirror now who do you see? Looking back at the questions from our initial discovery, reflect again on what you want people to say about you, what you want your strengths to be, and what success looks like for you. We must revisit these big questions in a timeline that works best for us to live without regrets.

What Goals Are Next?

 JOT IT Write down your ideas for the next six months ahead. Let's build upon the progress that you have made so far. Take a minute to jot it down now. Capture One to Two Ideas – Details Related to These Goals with Specific Action Steps with Timeframes

Specific Action Items	How Measured	Related To/ Contingent On	By When

Anticipating the (Un)expected: Transitions, Crisis, and Planning Ahead

Knowing yourself, how you respond to transitions or crises, and even how you react to long-term planning is helpful. So often, after working with a client through the 4D process, we then tackle some of these bigger topics. It is always helpful to think about the long game of life and all the unexpected things that may come along in your journey. While we have our sturdy boat with precise destinations outlined, unexpected things always come up along the way. We cannot predict the storms and the surprises that are part of life. So, make a plan and prepare for the unexpected as best as we can.

TRANSITIONS

Life is one perpetual transition, and it is helpful to meet each one with full awareness, whether it is expected or a surprise. Transition points are the most common times to seek or search for meaning in our work. They test our strength and resilience and challenge us to consider if we want to continue on one path or move to another. We have many transitions throughout life: elementary school to high school, college, first job, career advancement, parenting, aging, midlife (crisis/opportunity), senior leadership, and so on; you get it. For some, we start on a path and keep moving forward.

I have worked with many executives who started their career path after college and have kept climbing the corporate ladder, never looking back. Often, though, the mindset of having the "big" job might land a client stuck on the corporate ladder, looking up but unable to climb forward. What if you do not see a natural inflection point? These intersections provide a forced time of reckoning and taking stock of our lives.

These intersections are gifts; they allow us to take inventory, take a breath, and truly consider what we want. We need to create them ourselves! This book has mimicked the experience for you. Picking up this book and engaging in this process has manufactured an inflection point, a perfect time for reflection and optimal planning. Avoid a path laden with regret. Autopilot is not the best course for moving through life. Rather, being intentional, identifying what we want going after it, and leveraging transition points to help us modify and align to our goals and our purpose will be more satisfying. If we determine living a life without regret is the ultimate path we aspire to, we must be conscious of our choices in each phase of life and of the consequences of our choices with our eyes wide open throughout our journey.

Sometimes, the question "What do you want?" puts us into an unnecessary tailspin of options and decisions. To pick a path forward, we also need the means to re-evaluate every so often. Sometimes, "What do you want?" seems like a forbidden question. If you have pursued an ambitious degree and have a full education and work experience to lean on and ride out for your entire career, then what? I have worked with attorneys, financial leaders, and small business owners who admit they would never choose their profession again, yet they are established and do not see any other choice. Life transitions often force a choice upon us, whether welcome or not. Transitions can be challenging and stretch us beyond our comfort and expectations because they come with the hard work of making decisions and taking risks.

 JOURNAL IT Think about a recent or upcoming transition. Consider what you want as the outcome and journal about it. Take three minutes to have this dialogue with yourself in your journal.

CRISIS

Sometimes, the best intentions and most thoughtful plans are interrupted by something unforeseen, something we cannot avoid or navigate around when an obstacle or circumstance blocks our path. We might be off and running, and life gets in the way with a crisis. The crisis can sometimes reveal the answers to our most important and valuable goals.

The Oxford Dictionary defines crisis as:

- "A time of intense difficulty, trouble, or danger"

- "A time when a difficult or important decision must be made"

This definition of crisis is broad and can apply to many. If you have lived through middle school or have parented a middle-school student as a pre-teen, you may have experienced this dictionary version of crisis. Middle school is often "a time of intense difficulty." For middle schoolers, not having an outfit for Halloween or not being invited to a birthday party or other celebration is their version of an age-appropriate crisis. I am attempting to introduce a little lightness here; however, we know from life experiences that we can build resilience and character when we face a crisis. It's not obvious at first that what strengthens and tests us builds our resilience. Crisis mode is sometimes hard for an extended period, with no light at the end of the tunnel. If you have gone through a divorce or the death of a parent or child, these are times of intense crisis mixed with grief. I hope you seek adequate support during these events and are surrounded by a community that can support you. The crisis we will address here relates to your career or life journey. If you are approaching your late 40s or recently turned 50, you may be experiencing the most famous, perhaps even cliché, midlife crisis, which is notorious for good reason!

You have been reading this book, which focuses on your learning and improvement, and you now have some well-practiced strategies for handling a crisis. Winston Churchill's quote has reverberated since he said "Never let a good crisis go to waste" to prompt resilient behavior. Leaders look for a silver lining in a crisis because dramatic change inevitably follows. There are opportunities for new ideas, growth, and innovative ways of operating. We can all improve how we face difficult situations, so let's cover a few strategies together.

First, self-awareness: know your automatic response. Some people seem hardwired to deal with a crisis, and some seem to panic when faced with the unexpected. Some people run toward the emergency, while others run away from an accident. Some are paralyzed and frozen in fear, not able to move forward. Look at yourself with curiosity, without judgment here, and witness your primary responses to stress from afar. How did you fare? Are there patterns in your response to a crisis? Some of our responses arise from nature, and some from nurture and how our life experiences shape our physical and emotional selves. There is no better or safer response to the crisis; how you react is noteworthy and provides information for you to prepare for the next seismic shift. Take a minute and think of a crisis you have faced.

In conflict, we all have hardwired personalities that dictate a first reaction of fight, flight, freeze, or fawn. We will define all four here. Think about that crisis you have faced. What was your reaction?

 JOT IT Circle one of the following:

Fight—take instant action, aggression, confrontation

Flight—ignore, dissociate, move, or run away

Freeze—feel paralyzed, unable to act, do nothing

Fawn—people pleasing to avoid conflict

Next, try to reengage your brain. When we react to a crisis, we may think we are on autopilot because the executive function portion of our brains, the prefrontal cortex, literally shuts down. Our brains have a profound survival response, whereas our brain enables us to focus on the more primordial functions of fight, flight, freeze, or fawn. So, when we talk about your current crisis, as your sounding board here—your coach—my goal is always for you to access and return to that rational brain region, the prefrontal cortex, to re-engage and reboot to help access better decision-making and identify what future actions are warranted.

We can get the logical brain back online by prompting questions requiring logical answers. A crisis often presents a problem we need to address before moving forward. Getting to the root cause of the problem is the natural first step. Sometimes, defining the problem is complex and complicated. Set yourself up for resolution by journaling. Do you have a crisis right now to consider?

 JOURNAL IT Consider pulling out your journal to logically consider the following questions:

- Define the problem exactly; what is your current crisis?

- Create safety—psychological safety or/and physical. What plan can help you feel safe?

- Explore options. Brainstorm with yourself or talk with a buddy about possible options.

- Establish support. Consider your support system of friends, family, or colleagues.

In conflict, we all have hardwired first reactions, and our awareness can help shape our intended response. With this knowledge, we can all learn about managing conflict to formulate common ground. We know there is a time to fight and a time to walk away. We also know that conflicts that are ignored often resurface as bigger, stronger issues down the line. So, face your conflict!

PLANNING AHEAD: YOUR FIVE-YEAR PLAN AND BEYOND

Where do you see yourself in five years?

Questions like this, however well-intentioned, may create undue anxiety for many of us. Offering up a vision for our future for another to evaluate—regardless of whether we are satisfied with our response—sets us up for scrutiny and evaluation. Can we make our thinking about what is next less stressful and more joyful?

This question is repeatedly asked again and again throughout your life—sometimes in a different format—but always with the same implication. In American society, we start children off young, asking them, "What do you want to be when you grow up?" and we enjoy the range of responses, which are realistic and fanciful. Soon, the questions become more serious, and the answers are held up and evaluated with greater scrutiny. We ask high school students, "Where do you want to go to college?" A few years later, the question becomes, "What do you want to declare as your major?" The questions continue throughout our careers. Your first job, where you want to live—the questions keep coming. You often wonder during your career if your current job is right for you or when you should change jobs or careers. Soon enough, the question will become, "What is your plan for retirement?"

All of these questions help us plot our course toward change and evolution. They echo my action-oriented approach, "Let's Go!" These questions can prompt anxiety as well. A better question might be "How do you want to spend your days, your free time, and your work time in the next five years?" or "What things do you do during the day that bring you energy and satisfaction?"

You may recognize my replacement questions, as they are similar to those we posed in the discovery section at the beginning of this book. I recommend you consider your values, why you work, and what success looks like as you face these questions. Your foundational values are helpful to consider as you answer these questions. I have included a Future Planning Template for you at the end of the book. You will notice that we have already covered every element in this process.

Debrief Highlights

Debrief is the phase where we learn from our experiences. Imagine sailing back from that destination and thinking about all of the elements of the trip: what went well? What would you do differently? This is the key time to learn and make adjustments, take notes for the next voyage ahead, and notice your emotions and energy. This is not the end of the journey, it is the key phase that feeds our next trip ahead. Our best learning is often through experience, and now is the time to consider what you have learned from your hard work.

 Debrief: Key Takeaways

- At this phase, measure your progress. What went well? What might you change?

- When were you in a flow state?

- What can you capture as you identify future goals?

- With a growth mindset, more neural synapses are possible, and our brains can adapt, reorganize, learn, and grow.

- Emotional intelligence differs from IQ. Emotional intelligence is something we can all improve!

- Understand your role in the conflict. Self-awareness and mastering self-regulation will help us avoid conflict or better manage when conflict occurs.

- Sharing intentions up front is an excellent strategy for avoiding conflict.

- Start-Stop-Continue is a tool to help you take inventory and capture your thinking.

- Acknowledge progress and recognize your efforts. Rewards and recognition create new habits as they reinforce optimal behavior.

- Transitions are plentiful in our complex lives—plan for them.

- A crisis will happen! Know how *you* react; prepare as best as you can

- Having a five-year plan, while daunting, is the best long game.

Making the Improvements Last: Healthy Practices

We have completed the process: Discover, Decide, Deliver, Debrief! This is a continuous improvement process, as your Debrief phase may lead directly to Discover again. You can continue identifying new goals and delivering on those as you grow. Each time we tackle something new, we may encounter roadblocks or barriers to progress. Keep the Deliver topics handy to review. Your work in the Discover phase can provide a foundation for years' worth of goals, so keep the energy and motivation high and build from your progress. You have this sturdy ship to help you explore future destinations, and you have gathered more experience by participating in this process. Take advantage of the channels you have created and keep chartering your chosen course until you arrive on the distant shore you envisioned.

You have learned about yourself and your barriers to success; you have learned about what works and what does not work as well for you at this stage in your development. You are not ending at the same place that you started. We are in a new spot together. Now, we will consider how to maintain this progress.

Health and Well-Being: Keeping the Progress Going

How do we keep the progress going? We make reflection a habit and try to repeat this process every six months or so, as needed. To set ourselves up for success, we need not be perfect. We have to hold ourselves accountable and take inventory now and then to keep ourselves on track.

Thank you for taking this journey with me. Before our work is complete, I have a few reminders for you as you move forward and continue this great energy and focus.

Once I help clients address a professional or personal goal and they experience the entire 4D process, inevitably there are bigger questions that arise.

At this point, I have to admit that I am an over-packer. When preparing for a journey, I plan ahead, carefully determine exactly what I need, and pack everything with care. At the last minute, I jam so many extra options in a carry-on bag in preparation for any weather, unexpected crisis, or even losing luggage.

 PACKING YOUR CARRY-ON BAG

I call this section the carry-on bag. It has everything that you might need handy in a travel size. It also includes many references for further reading if you really think you need the full size, not the travel size, for your journey ahead.

Up until this point, the process for Discover, Decide, Deliver, and Debrief has been pre-planned, step-by-step, and I hope clear. Rather than squish everything into this primary travel bag, I'm offering a separate duffel with some helpful topics, just in case one of these is something you personally need.

I call this section the *carry-on bag*. It has everything that you might need handy in a travel size. It also includes many references for further reading if you really think you need the full size, not the travel size, for your journey ahead.

Your personal health and well-being are the center of your ability to sustain success.

Many clients will build trust and reveal to me a true vulnerability or personal struggle with one or several of these fundamental elements. It could be a mental health issue, a family-related crisis, a recent diagnosis, or anything that is in better hands with a trained professional to address. I am including this section to briefly cover each of these "big picture" elements with resources identified that I have shared with my clients.

Each of these topics has fields of research and expertise that are readily available. I am sharing high-level overviews of each in this section for you if you are interested in an introduction to any of these topics.

You are at the helm; you are the captain.

Sustaining good habits for your health and well-being will benefit your entire life journey. Sleep, exercise, fuel, mindfulness, relationships, and stress are all connected. As you steer toward your next goal, consider these for a successful journey.

- Sleep
- Exercise
- Mindfulness

- Food
- Stress Management
- Relationships

The Carry-On Bag: Habits for Health: Mental, Physical, Spiritual, and Emotional

When we think of our health and longevity, do we automatically think about mental, physical, spiritual, and emotional health? We will take a moment to review and look at all these instrumental components. A healthy body and sound mind will lead to our productivity and longevity.

There are endless resources to address our spiritual and mental health. Most of us are just a quick Google or app search away from answers to our questions on topics related to our mental and physical states. There is growing research on the impacts of spiritual and emotional fitness as it affects every aspect of how we show up for ourselves, our families, at work, and in communities. While the advice is plentiful, I attempt to capture some basic thoughts here that have served my clients well. These are the plain, straightforward truths. They may not be new to you, but your commitment to them might be new, especially after getting to the end of this book with new insights.

Specifically, we will cover the topics of sleep, food, exercise, stress management, mindfulness, and relationships. Each of these topics has a complete body of work to explore. Do not hesitate to sail directly into a topic until you discover a pearl of wisdom to bring with you on your voyage. Although I do not provide an exhaustive list, I have included resources to inspire greater research and reflection in each section. This book has been intended as your guide, with a compass pointing toward your true north and a conduit to spark further discovery.

Sleep, nutrition, and exercise cover the trifecta of health. These elements are paramount when we visit our doctor for an annual exam. Too often, we look at the lagging indicators for our health, blood work results, or a disease diagnosis, and then we wonder, what prompted this outcome? Too often, the mental and physical preventative measures within our control fail to motivate. We wait until something hurts or we cannot function at our usual capacity. Before it is too late, consider the inputs, the leading indicators in your life, and the built-in habits formed around them. To accelerate your success, consider these essentials.

HABITS FOR HEALTH: SLEEP

While this topic lands more in the personal realm than the work zone, no one argues that sleep directly affects our professional performance. Unfortunately, the data regarding manifesting work performance issues became apparent only after exposing sleep deprivation as a contributing factor. The consequences of sleep deprivation are difficult to measure. When a successful business leader creates excellent outcomes, we never acknowledge the advantage of prioritizing uninterrupted sleep! We all understand, intuitively, without data, how operating on inadequate sleep affects us personally. We know from the news reports how sleep deprivation results in train derailments, traffic accidents, medical missteps, and more. We learn from trial and error that our patience is less, our caffeine intake may spike, and long-term sleep deprivation seriously impacts our health.

Our ability to recoup our daily mental energy is foundational to everything else. If we have a good sleep, then everything builds from there. Before you start on future goals, consider clocking in more hours of sleep so you're not starting with a half-full tank each day and trying to manage. Easier said than done, yet there are many factors to consider when questioning why we may not sleep well. Please investigate the barriers preventing you from getting good quality sleep and address them.

In her *New York Times* bestseller *The Sleep Revolution*, Arianna Huffington shares the impact of our productivity-driven society's dismissal of the importance of sleep. Huffington has been on a crusade to bring attention to the critical issue of sleep for our overall physical health, general brain function, and mental and emotional well-being. Huffington, cofounder and editor-in-chief of the *Huffington Post* shifted her focus to highlight the impacts of sleep deprivation based on her personal experience of sacrificing sleep to focus on her professional success. She experienced the dire consequences of depriving herself of much-needed sleep. Her research is impressive. "According to a recent Gallup poll, 40 percent of all American adults are sleep-deprived, clocking significantly less than the recommended minimum of seven hours of sleep per night."[32]

No doubt about it, sleep is the cornerstone of our health. "Getting enough sleep," says Dr. Judith Owens, the Center for Pediatric Sleep Disorders director at Boston Children's Hospital, is "just as important as good nutrition, physical activity, and wearing your seatbelt."[33] In fact, so essential for our brain health.

"…Scientists are resoundingly confirming what our ancestors knew instinctively: that our sleep is not empty time. Sleep is a time of intense neurological activity—a rich time of renewal, memory consolidation, brain and neurochemical cleansing, and cognitive maintenance. Properly appraised, our sleeping time is as valuable a commodity as the time we are awake. In fact, getting the right amount of sleep enhances the quality of every minute we spend with our eyes open."[34] The practice of going to sleep when it is dark and waking when the sun rises is foreign to many. Our ancestors knew how essential our connection to the rhythms of nature was to optimal human function. Modern life does not lend itself to this necessity.

🗎 CLIENT PEEK

It is common for me to troubleshoot poor sleep with my clients, as many leaders have confided in me that sleep is one of their biggest barriers to peak performance. While some of my clients troubleshoot the sleepless nights, one of my clients often boasted about their ability to excel at their job on little sleep. They shared play-by-plays of "all-nighters" with me and intense deadlines where they compromised sleep to meet their business goals. Even when I provided evidence and research contradicting these beliefs, they met the evidence skeptically.

Events turned when they welcomed their first baby. I could only dig in and discuss strategies for delegating tasks and streamlining work to prioritize sleep. Once the baby amplified the need for change, researched strategies and ideas were quickly implemented. Like Huffington, sometimes we need to experience that inflection point to make a change. I encourage you to address any sleep dilemmas before you reach an inflection point or crisis of your own.

Think about your commitment to your sleep. Did you sleep well last night? Consider how much sleep is essential to our well-being and performance. Is this an area where you need to set a new goal? Some subscribe to the tongue and cheek mantra, "I'll sleep when I'm dead." Unfortunately, this motto fails to recognize that it will not provide the benefits of sleep now, in our current roles, and with our current goals.

HABITS FOR HEALTH: GOOD-QUALITY FOOD

Like sleep, quality food is not optional. We use food daily to sustain ourselves, so selecting the right fuel is essential.

Michael Pollan, journalist and bestselling author, provides some direction through his book *The Omnivore's Dilemma*. Pollen's book has stood the test of time. He instructs, "Eat real food, not too much, mostly plants." His advice includes shopping around the outer isles of the grocery store, daily fresh fruit, vegetables, and eating proteins that are readily available, and skipping the processed packaged food in the middle aisles. Pollan provides practical insight to help consumers understand where food comes from, how food comes to market, and what to consider when making healthier food choices.[35]

Think about this topic and how it applies to you. How is the quality of your food affecting you? Does your doctor, the scale, your gut, or your skin provide any indication of how things are going for you related to food? You probably know from the inside out if you have a health issue. Close your eyes. How does your body feel? Addressing your food supply is imperative to change your general quality of health.

> If you have a known diagnosis or a special diet you could be following and can't seem to make it happen, pick up my friend Marissa Costonis' book, *Change Bites*. In it, she helps you learn how to change your eating to preserve your health. Her book is a wonderful resource if you need to change your diet for better outcomes.

Think about your own health and if you need to investigate the many resources related to understanding what nutrition might work best for you.

HABITS FOR HEALTH: EXERCISE

Exercise, in any form, is going to make us feel better. Simply taking a walk or elevating our heart rate changes our body chemistry. We all know exercise is good for us, yet some still do not put exercise time on the calendar. Just like a good night's sleep, daily exercise is something we need to prioritize if we expect ourselves to operate at peak levels. Exercise is not something that we can delegate or outsource; we need to commit to it ourselves!

The Centers for Disease Control and Prevention posted on its website in 2023, "Physical activity is anything that gets your body moving." According to the current government website on the Physical Activity Guidelines for Americans, the guidelines state that adults need 150 minutes of moderate-intensity physical activity each week and two days of muscle-strengthening activity.[36]

While the studies are also sometimes contradictory regarding exercise and weight loss, with many ideas proven and then disproven over time, one thing is clear: moving helps our physical and mental health and is associated with lowering stress levels. We know how exercise makes us feel, so the following is no surprise: "Some of the benefits of physical activity on brain health occur immediately after a session of moderate-to-vigorous physical activity. With regular physical activity, improvements are seen in anxiety, deep sleep, and components of executive function."[37] As I am writing this, numerous studies are being conducted to connect physical exercise with brain health. The bottom line is that exercise is good for us and makes us feel good.

Many clients and colleagues share that they exercise for stress reduction. Exercise becomes a coping method for dealing with the day's anxieties or the week's stress. Physiologically, aerobic exercise increases respiration by oxygenating our blood. A simple walk will help decrease cortisol levels, the stress hormone.

For some of my clients who are willing, I offer to meet for "walk and talk" meetings. More successful interactions have occurred during this non-traditional method of meeting. Consider adding exercise into your workday by adding a walk (or a walking meeting), a lunchtime workout, or 10-minute bursts of physical activity between appointments. Exercise can take many forms, and it helps the mind and body manage our daily lives with more clarity, focus, and composure. Exercise will help you sleep better and may even inspire healthier food choices.

HABITS FOR HEALTH: RELATIONSHIPS AND EMOTIONAL WELLNESS

Accepting ourselves and our interdependence with others enhances our lives. Emotional wellness affects our relationship with ourselves and others in our communities.

People often link the feeling of love with the feeling of happiness. However, for many reasons, this association is problematic, if fleeting. Love is difficult to define aptly. Its simplified definition as "an intense feeling of deep affection" does not express the depth and complexity related to levels of human connection and their associated emotional states.[38] A dictionary definition of love doesn't paint the full picture. *Time Magazine* published in February 2016 an article entitled "We Are Defining Love the Wrong Way," and the author, Rabbi David Wolpe, suggests that love is to act in a certain way, a "loving" way.[39] Our emotional well-being, however, is not limited to having loving relationships. Sometimes, love brings feelings of heartbreak, depression, and loss. The National Institutes of Health (NIH) describes emotional well-being as "the ability to successfully handle life's stresses and adapt to change and difficult times."[40] So, how do we improve our emotional well-being?

The NIH publishes the following strategies for improving your emotional health in its Emotional Wellness toolkit. It seems that many toolkits refer to similar things. These tools should look familiar based on what we have already covered:

- Build resilience   Reduce stress

- Get quality sleep   Strengthen social connections

- Cope with loss   Be mindful

I tend to learn a lot of personal details about my clients, their families, and their challenges. My approach is to understand the whole picture of my clients' experiences. If there is an ailing relationship at the root cause of poor performance at work, that must be part of the conversation in addressing any future goal.

You will continue to see that toolkits for our overall health have many crossovers, whether they are focused on mental health or physical health; the research frequently outlines suggestions that overlap. The hardest element I have faced with clients has been coping with loss. Loss is something that individuals truly need to process themselves. I have been fortunate to be supportive for some dealing with loss. Relationships help with loss; having someone to lean on and someone who listens brings comfort and helps with grief.

Think about your relationships. Are there areas where you can strengthen your presence with someone in your immediate circle? When facing a personal crisis or helping someone else with theirs, being heard and able to listen actively is a great first step in being supported or receiving support.

 JOT IT Consider your current relationships. Who do you want to make time for on your calendar for the upcoming month? Write it down, or even better, pull out your calendar and schedule it!

Stress and Cortisol: Addressing Both for Health

Life, and certainly loss, brings on stress. Stress is known to impact health. Identifying proven strategies for coping with stress is important, and knowing what tools work best for you will make your journey more accessible.

We already covered the topic of *crisis*. Now, we know the biological impact of stressors and how they affect our brains. Adrenaline and cortisol levels rise in the body, and the brain and body prepare for fight, flight, freeze, or fawn. Our nervous system and our supporting systems all change to address perceived threats.

While this chain reaction serves us well for a tiger attack, this physical response to a project deadline or an angry boss will take its toll over the long term. The Mayo Clinic addresses the impact of cortisol and stress on the body and identifies the potential outcomes of long-term stress. Mayo Clinic warns that the long-term activation of the stress response system and overexposure to cortisol and other stress hormones can disrupt almost all of your body's processes.[41] Long-term stress and high cortisol levels can result in the following medical issues: anxiety, depression, digestive problems, headaches, muscle tension and pain, heart disease, heart attack, high blood pressure, stroke, sleep problems, weight gain, memory impairment, concentration impairment, and more.

We can argue that some stress is good. "Eustress" results when the adrenaline junkie climbs a mountain and gets a rush to achieve their goal. The negative outcomes apply when the stress does not relent when we experience prolonged and sustained levels of stress that result in high cortisol levels.

 CLIENT PEEK

In my coaching practice, nearly every client I have worked with reports high-stress levels at some point. I often meet them when they have recently experienced a crisis, which is their initial reason for contacting me. Talking to a colleague and working through a stressful event is a key coping strategy. Once, I had a long-term client call me, and all we did during our meeting was breathe together. If you are stressed, getting some deep breaths into your lungs is an excellent first step. I have also had successful outcomes from working with clients through some coping methods described next.

HABITS FOR HEALTH: COPING METHODS FOR MANAGING STRESS

Stress is one of our biggest challenges. In the late 1990s, stress management was a topic that was finally addressed in corporate America, with many organizations focused on how to bring resources to employees who faced high stress levels. Stress management was one of the training classes I taught in my professional development curriculum. Now, there are resources you can quickly find on the internet, and stress reduction programs to launch right from your smartphone.

The part of our brain that reacts to stress does not naturally address a given situation's logic or rationality. As mentioned, our brain reacts and generally reverts to a "fight or flight" state. To counteract the acute stress response, use strategies that tap into the executive functioning brain, the prefrontal cortex. We can achieve this in many different ways.

Consider trying one or many of these strategies for stress reduction:

- **Change your internal physiology**: Any activity that helps release endorphins will change your physiology. Walking, exercising, taking a shower or bath, swimming, and going outside into nature all help when you are stressed.

- **Breathing technique to engage executive function in your brain**: Inhale to the count of five as you put each finger up from a …. 1-2-3-4-5. Then, exhale to the count of five, putting the fingers back down with each number, tapping your palm. This technique triggers the parasympathetic nervous system and allows us to move out of fight or flight, engaging the prefrontal cortex to remember your count and tap each finger. Although this breathing technique is simple, it redirects your brain and is quite effective.[42]

- **Distract the anxiety loop**: Never underestimate the power of distraction. Getting your brain to focus on something else, look at the horizon, or toward something different than your anxiety or the problem that brought on your stress response in the first place. Read a book, watch an uplifting show, or call a friend—each activity will distract your brain from the stress cycle.

- **Go outside**: Getting fresh air, taking a break in nature, and noticing the natural world around you will improve and strengthen your resolve. A trip outside sounds good for everything— increased happiness, well-being, social interactions, and a sense of life purpose. Do not hesitate to go outside right now and take a stroll! Good leaders know when to take a break. Get outside and connect with "forest bathing," or if you don't have access to a forest, get on the roof of your building and look up at the sky and watch the birds fly by. Your brain and body will thank you as you appreciate a perspective-altering moment in the sun!

CLIENT PEEK

Once, I led an entire executive team outside for a walk in silence in the middle of a merger planning discussion. The conference room had become tense, and we reached a sticking point in our strategic planning discussion. So, I instructed the team to get into a single file line and walk outside around the building in silence. Try this with your team; the mental space we gained during the walk shifted the energy completely when we returned to the conference room.

When we step outside, we reconnect with nature as part of our internal experience—engaging all five senses. Under artificial lighting and recirculated air, our minds and bodies don't function the same as if we can take a moment to recalibrate in the natural world. Immersing ourselves in the green grass and using our senses is a concept introduced to manage stress.[43]

Finding meaning through immersion in the natural world was brought mainstream through Henry David Thoreau's book Walden. His novel was published in 1854 and is still studied in universities today as an example of the deep reverence we feel for a peaceful place to reconnect with ourselves. Thoreau sought to find the meaning of life by living in the woods for over two years, surrounding himself with nature to find the answers he sought. His famous quote directs us, "Rather than love, than money, than fame, give me truth."[44] He writes about his quest to discover the truth in this novel that resonates with us today. Perhaps even more so, as many of us spend most of our work lives indoors.

- **Talk it out:** Sometimes, discussing our stress with friends or colleagues allows us to vocalize the details of our day. Stress can sound different when we hear ourselves process it out loud. The stress dissipates and doesn't sound as bad as when we ruminate by ourselves in our heads.

 JOURNAL IT Consider if you don't have anyone to process with, you can ask yourself questions with your inner voice. These questions might help you look at your situation more clearly:

- What is the worst outcome?

- What is the likelihood of that happening?

- What is the best outcome or resolution to this crisis?

- What is the probability of this happening—a percentage?

- **Stay in balance with healthy habits:** Finally, creating a life where you feel a sense of control and balance is most helpful. Everyday stressors will impact you less if you have enough sleep, eat well, and take the time to care for yourself. All the elements mentioned, sleep, food, and exercise, will help regulate your stress.

HABITS FOR HEALTH: MEDITATION

Practicing mindfulness and meditation are key strategies for strengthening our ability to handle stress. Consider building the habit of adding some meditation into your day or your week. These ancient practices can be used as antidotes to our modern-day problems. While their usefulness as spiritual practices, applied to Buddhism, for example, has been commonly accepted, their application for pain management and influencing personal success is more of a modern finding.

We cannot deny the connection between the mind and the body. Gabor Maté and Daniel Maté include in their book, *The Myth of Normal: Trauma, Illness, and Healing in a Toxic Culture* that the mind-body connection is the link between our nonphysical thoughts, attitudes, and patterns of behavior and our physical body and physical health. It is a cornerstone of holistic medicine that treats the whole person in mind, body, and spirit, not just individual symptoms. There is solid scientific evidence—as well as many long-standing traditional philosophies—that our thoughts have powerful effects on our bodies, and our bodies can influence our patterns of thought.[45] This connection makes us conscious partners in our healing, performance, and overall wellness systems.

What Exactly Is Mindful Meditation?

If you are new to meditation or have never tried yoga, consider this easy introduction to meditation. When you sit in silence, your mind drifts. When you have a thought, remind yourself to bring awareness back to your breath. Have the thought, let this thought go, and wait for the next thought to arise. In the meantime, refocus on your breath. Practice brings your conscious mind back to paying attention to your breath. Welcome to mindfulness!

The benefits are plentiful, including working on "non-distraction." The goal would be to practice mindfulness and make this state your default mode instead of being in a general state of mindlessness. Notice what your mind's eye is seeing at this moment. Now, you are back in the present moment. You can begin again, and your access to awareness grows in the present moment. The biggest misconception about practicing yoga or mindfulness is that people think the goal is to keep their minds blank. Thought will arise, but the more you practice, the more space you can cultivate between your thoughts. Continue to bring your attention back to your breath or the present moment.

Meditation, Mindfulness, Present Moment: Want to Know More?

Mindfulness and meditation, two practices that have been studied for their benefits for mental health and pain management, might be the most ancient of the practices we are considering. While meditation and mindfulness practices have recently become more mainstream in American culture, with the increased focus on mental health since the global pandemic, these practices may be the earliest practices of all that contribute to sustaining our health. The earliest documented records to include meditation are from India around 1500 BCE. Yet historians believe that meditation was possibly first practiced as early as 3000 BCE.

Mindfulness and meditation have brought ancient practices to modern-day problems we face. While their usefulness as spiritual practices, like Buddhism, has been commonly accepted, their application for pain management and for influencing personal success is more of a modern finding. As *Time Magazine* reported in a 2003 cover story, "How Meditation Went Mainstream," meditation began to be seriously studied for its medical benefits in the 1960s when a researcher in India named B.K. Anand "found that yogis could meditate themselves into trances so deep that they didn't react when hot test tubes were pressed against their arms."[46]

Jon Kabat-Zinn, the father of modern-day mindfulness, started developing mindfulness-based stress reduction (MBSR) in 1979 in the basement of the University of Massachusetts Medical Center, where he taught patients in chronic pain how to meditate. "He believed that patients needed to be active participants in their own healing, and he was right. He found that those who received mindfulness meditation training had much better health outcomes." Zinn says that mindfulness is the heart of meditation. Mindfulness is awareness. Zinn has this specific, complete definition for further clarity: "The awareness of paying attention on purpose, in the present moment without judgment."[47]

Today, Zinn's techniques for stress reduction are more mainstream and used in hospitals worldwide. Zinn has proven that mindfulness helps alleviate pain and can also strengthen our ability to face stress and stressful situations. Breathing practices, such as meditation and yoga, have all been proven to help. I have had many clients who tell me that they just cannot sit in silence and meditate. So, I suggest yoga, as yoga connects meditation with movement. A guided meditation that you can download on an app on your cell phone works, too. Breath is "a very powerful door into the present moment," and if you experience breath, moment by moment, you are meditating!

Now that you know how to meditate, what is breathwork?

When you sit in silence, your mind drifts. When you have this thought, you remind yourself to come back to paying attention just to your breath. Have the thought, let it go. The practice is bringing yourself back to paying attention to your breath. This is practicing mindfulness. Zinn says, "It is the hardest work in the world, and it is also the easiest work in the world."[48] Now you are practicing breathwork!

How are you using this present moment?

Reading this book is a great use of your mindfulness today!

Full Circle: Success, Happiness, and Fulfillment

Our last topic to tackle is happiness. One of my clients came to me with this simple request: "Can you write a book about how to find happiness?" As I shared with him at the time, I have studied happiness, and I know for sure that only *you* can define what the key to happiness is for you. Just as the title of this book reflects, your success is yours, defined by you, and accomplished by you. Now, we find ourselves back at the beginning, in our same roles. You are the expert on you; I am the guide. This whole process is intended to help you accelerate and move faster to find your own unique success. Is happiness the same as success? Is fulfillment? Let's investigate this moving target together. We are not the first professionals to get curious and explore these profound topics. Work-life balance and the happiness equation are an art to maintain and a place we may discover only to lose again.

WHAT IS THE KEY TO HAPPINESS?

What is happiness? What creates happiness?

Happiness and fulfillment are not necessarily interchangeable. Be specific when describing a desired life outcome.

Happiness is defined differently, depending on who you ask.

In *A New Earth*, Eckhart Tolle writes, "The secret to happiness" is "making peace with the present moment...the field on which the game of life happens." He elaborates, "There are three words that convey the secret of the art of living, the secret of all success and happiness: One with Life. Being one with life is being one with Now."[49]

This directive, the present moment, seems to surface as an essential element to finding happiness. Happiness lives in the now, not in the future, where the goal line keeps moving further and further out of reach. Consider working on happiness as a daily commitment to making peace with the present moment. If you like daily reminders, like the pages of a calendar, consider Gretchen Rubin's book, *The Happiness Project*.

Gretchen Rubin's work entitled *The Happiness Project* follows her for a calendar year as she takes on strategies, tries new things, and establishes habits aligning with health and well-being. If you are looking for a step-by-step daily guide to creating happiness, check out her book and calendar.

We know that happiness is active; it takes effort. Just as we build awareness about managing our stress, we can also build habits that increase our happiness.

Csikszentmihalyi insists, "...happiness does not simply happen." He asserts, "...people must prepare for happiness—cultivated by each person— "by setting challenges that are neither too demanding nor too simple for one's abilities."[50]

Take a minute to explore this essential topic for yourself. Jot down your thoughts here, pull out your journal, or simply take an honest look in the mirror today to explore this.

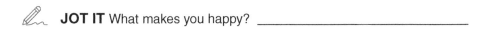 **JOT IT** What makes you happy? _____

JOURNAL IT Take note of what makes you happy, when you were happiest in your life, and what your inner thoughts are about pursuing more happiness.

 REFLECT Ask yourself in the mirror. Is there a difference between being happy and being successful or even fulfilled?

Happiness is just one of the key elements for living a fulfilled life. What we know for certain is that these words represent different components of our lives. Purpose, engagement, or achievement alone may not equate with happiness. As we gain more years on this planet, we may contemplate the differences and connections between these words with acute awareness.

HAPPINESS VS. SUCCESS

In my experience, happiness is frequently equated with levels of success. The word *achievement* aligns with many corporate definitions of how successful we are within monetary or social collateral standards.

Many clients tell me, "I'll be happy when…" about reaching certain financial or promotion-based goals. Research on happiness has found that our measure of happiness does not equate to goal achievement, financial success, or other traditional measures society defines as "success."

> Shawn Achor wrote in *The Happiness Advantage* that happiness fuels success, not the other way around. Achor introduces his book with the following observation: "If you observe the people around you, you'll find most individuals follow a formula that has been subtly or not so subtly taught to them by their schools, their company, their parents, or society. That is, If you work hard, you will become successful, and then you'll be happy…..Success first, and happiness second. The only problem is that this formula is broken."[51]

We cannot assume that people work to make money and that making money equates to a successful life. There are numerous examples of wealthy people who are depressed or publicly unhappy. Wealth does not insulate us from seeking and searching for a happier life or thinking about how to maintain our equilibrium. Life's meaning is often associated with wisdom. Consumer culture supports limitless desire, even fear that we can never have enough. What is enough for you?

COULD YOU BE HAPPIER?

In this process, the key is to find your definition of personal, whole-pie success and, by extension, your version of happiness. Some of us have a happier baseline than others. You may know colleagues who seem gloomy or others who always seem more positive. Research has proven some humans are genetically happier than others, with 972 genes potentially involved in making us happy. [52]Yet, nature versus nurture comes into consideration with the solid argument suggesting our free will as humans and the freedom of choice. We can create our own happiness and well-being. Personality, access to education, resources, social advantages, and even gratitude influence our capacity to experience contentment in our professional and personal lives.

While I agree that our personalities may or may not be predisposed to look for the half-full glass or half-empty, our brain is set up to look for threats and has a negativity bias. I have worked my whole career to help people move toward the growth mindset, the nurturing side of themselves and identify how they could bring more joy, satisfaction, and, ultimately, happiness into their lives.

If this is something you would like to explore further, consider reading *The Book of Joy* by His Holiness, The Dalai Lama and Archbishop Desmond Tutu. You will benefit from the collective wisdom of these two Nobel Prize winners and spiritual leaders as they present their experiences with joyful living. They have been role models practicing and promoting self-awareness and many of the skills illustrated in this book.

FULFILLMENT: MEANING AND PURPOSE

Happiness is not tied directly to goal achievement but rather to the identity we create as we accomplish our goals. Our vision of who we want to become actually fuels the driving force of happiness—precisely why we started at the beginning of this process, defining what success looks like for *you*.

Instead of asking, "Are you happy?" we may ask, "Do you have purpose and meaning, engagement, great relationships, and fulfillment in your life?" Meaning, purpose, and values provide and compel our direction. This customized look at who we hope to become amplifies our satisfaction when we get there. We can recognize and embrace happiness when we acknowledge the hard work of becoming more authentically who we have wanted to be. Our evolving identity, the one we sought all along, was waiting for us to arrive.

As with this process, I prompt questions, and you must provide the answers. Your journey is like no other. At different phases of our lives, we prioritize things differently. What success looks like to *you* right *now* is unique to you. Success is living your life by your definition of your authentic self.

Final Thoughts: Your Authentic Self

"Be yourself; everyone else is already taken." —Oscar Wilde

If there is one concept that I share with every single client I have worked with over the past three decades, it is to make sure they bring their authentic self to work each day. Too often, we look outside of ourselves to consider what we should be doing instead of looking inside at our intentions and strengths. That does not mean we can't become a better version of ourselves; we can! We can still set goals, try new behaviors, and practice new habits for better outcomes.

 CLIENT PEEK

I worked with a client who "altered" his natural tendencies and put on the cloak of his impression of an executive each day. Like a chameleon, he would show up in the office daily to fit the mold of his definition of a "successful executive." He described this as leaving behind this easygoing, "Type B" person to become the assertive "Type A" version. This was, however, not a success. His "Type A" cloak was surprising to his colleagues. His co-workers were surprised when he had unpredictable outbursts in meetings or when he took a stand on things that seemed out of character. When we uncovered his intention behind the behavior, he realized he was trying to appear strong and decisive by imitating an assertive leadership style that did not suit him. Coaching him to be his true self, the easygoing, funny, witty, competent, self-described "Type B" leader, was when he made the breakthroughs in his performance. Colleagues all around him began to reciprocate his relationship-building efforts, and he excelled in his work and personal life.

When we try to take on attributes that do not align with our identity and values, we invite trouble. It is much more effective to be straightforward, be yourself, and respect the diversity of styles of those around you. When we try to conform to a version of ourselves that skirts authenticity, our behavior will inevitably give us away.

I suggest you bring your unique strengths, beliefs, and true personality to your work life and ensure you share your intentions, act in alignment with your values, and continue to learn. A growth mindset serves us well. Being who we truly are, having the freedom to spend our time doing things we love, inhabiting the flow state more often, and doing work that brings fulfillment and satisfaction create the ultimate success stories!

Conclusion

Thank you for taking this journey.

Awareness alone does not prompt change. If this were the case, everyone would exercise, no one would smoke or misuse drugs, and healthy eating would be the norm. It takes more than knowing the facts to prompt change. We need to do the work. Together, we pushed to clarify your *why*—the deep reasons for change that are connected to our identity. We examined our mindset, how our brains work, and how our self-talk can be an asset or hindrance. We looked at our styles and preferences. We examined how our physiology helps us make changes as we experience endorphins associated with action and accomplishment. The release of dopamine in our bodies as we cross the finish line of another task completion reinforces our desire to rise to meet the next goal.

Starting together in discovery and answering the big questions, deciding on goals, delivering outcomes, and looking back to evaluate ourselves is a robust process. We see the benefits of changing our behavior and acting on our goals. The intention alone is never enough, nor is establishing the task list. Committing is not enough either. Over time, practice, effort, and repetition help us move effectively toward our desired life. Acknowledging progress, no matter how small, helps us continue the forward motion. We must reflect and debrief to have the confidence to persevere, reestablish new targets, and look for improvement areas. Thank you for taking this journey with me. Keep up the "Let's Go!" attitude. I wish you true success, growing fulfillment, and authentic happiness.

Future Planning Template

You now have all of the elements to continue this process and plan for longer-term success. Remember, you define what success looks like for you! You have already done the heavy lifting, and now you may use your Discover, Decide, Deliver, Debrief awareness to look into your future with confidence.

From the Discover Process, you have your sturdy boat hull. Capture it here:

Strengths _____

Preferences _____

Style _____

Why You Work _____

Success _____

Values _____

You

Sturdy Foundation The hull of your
ship for this journey

Roles: Reflect back on page 64, where you looked at your roles and created your current and future pie. Revisit them here:

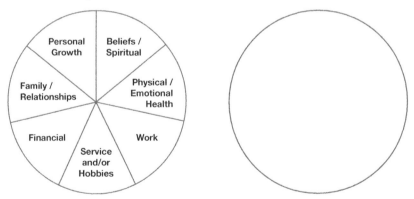

Personal Growth / Beliefs / Spiritual / Family / Relationships / Physical / Emotional Health / Financial / Service and/or Hobbies / Work

SMART Goals Near Term: Think about your roles and identify some longer-term goals. Remember your Start-Stop-Continue chart on page 108 in Debrief? What do you want to change? Consider the timeframe of a year to five years ahead. Capture your roles with the corresponding goals on the next page.

Roles	Targets (Goals)

SMART Goals Long Term: Go ahead, dream big, and think about your future. What long-term goals do you aspire to? Capture them here.

1. _____

2. _____

3. _____

Expand Your Toolkit: It has been an honor to be your guide so far and to prompt you to work with a buddy, your journal, or to reflect in the mirror. Now, think about expanding your tool kit. Capture your thinking here.

Network (List the people to talk with as mentors/ advisors/ influencers)

1. _____

2. _____

3. _____

Research (Learning along the way is essential. I have included reference books for you to consider, and the resources you can tap are endless! What will you investigate to accomplish these goals?)

1. _____

2. _____

3. _____

Celebrate Milestones: Remember to identify targets and milestone points so you can see all that you have accomplished as you go. Celebrate when you can! Keep your foot on the accelerator; your own definition of success is just ahead. You control the speed for this work. Your circle of control and your mindset, habits and tools are all aligned for your success. Thank you for taking this journey with me!

Recommended Reading

These are some of the books I've mentioned that I often suggest to my clients. If you want to learn more about the topics I've introduced, I recommend these authors.

- Simon Sinek. *Start with Why: How Great Leaders Inspire Everyone to Take Action*

- Buckingham, M., & Clifton, D. O. *Now, Discover Your Strengths.* New York, Free Press

- Cain, Susan. *Quiet: The Power of Introverts in a World That Can't Stop Talking*

- Frankl, Viktor E. *Man's Search for Meaning: An Introduction to Logotherapy.*

- Gladwell, Malcolm. *Outliers: The Story of Success*

- Richardson, Cheryl. *Take Time for Your Life*

- Senge, Peter. *The Fifth Discipline*

- Dweck, PH.D., Carol S. *Mindset: The New Psychology of Success*

- Jenniges, Sam. *Recognition Rebooted*

- Buckingham, Marcus. *Love + Work How to Find What You Love, Love What You Do, and Do It for the Rest of Your Life*

- Bradberry, Travis, and Jean Greaves. *Emotional Intelligence 2.0*

- Clear, James. *Atomic Habits: Tiny Changes, Remarkable Results: An Easy and Proven Way to Build Good Habits and Break Bad Ones*

- Huffington, Arianna. *The Sleep Revolution: Transforming Your Life, One Night at a Time*

- Pollan, Michael. 2011. *The Omnivore's Dilemma: A Natural History of Four Meals*

- Costonis, Marissa. *Change Bites: 5 Change Management Strategies to Transform Your Health*

- Thoreau, Henry David. *Walden*

- Tolle, Eckhart. *A New Earth, Awakening Your Life's Purpose*

- Rubin, Gretchen. *The Happiness Project*

- Achor, Shawn. *The Happiness Advantage: The Seven Principles of Positive Psychology That Fuel Success and Performance at Work*

- Covey, Stephen. T*he 7 Habits of Highly Effective People*

- His Holiness, The Dalai Lama, and Archbishop Desmond Tutu. *The Book of Joy: Lasting Happiness in a Changing World*

Acknowledgments

This book was inspired by my neighbor and so many other people who had reached out to me when they needed a sounding board. It is a gift to be trusted to listen to internal struggles as we journey through life.

To all of my clients, thank you for trusting me with your thoughts and feelings and for engaging with the improvement process. I will always maintain your confidence, and I hope you are proud of some of the examples from our conversations in this book. Your experiences are helping others!

When Cigdem Knebel approached me after I delivered a presentation on Confidence and casually mentioned that she would be interested in reading my book, I had no idea that her support, encouragement, and masterful guidance would result in an actual book. Thanks, Cigdem, for nudging me along this path with all your edits, phone calls, and direction every step of the way.

To my BFF colleague, business partner, and lifelong friend, Sam Jenniges, I am in awe of you and have been learning from you since we met. Your generosity with your time, ideas, and direction is unmatched.

To Marissa Costonis, my accountability buddy in real life, thank you for your weekly check-in calls and your diligent attention to my outline. I'm so glad that this project finally got past the outline phase. You continue to make it look easy! To Christy for her check-ins and timely advice on this publishing roller coaster and for her advice to Just Go!

To my amazingly patient editors, Dondi Tondro-Smith and Kim Wimpsett, thank you for your diligent eyes. Thank you to my talented artist, Michelle Fairbanks for the cover and to my incredible interiors, Jessica Trippe. To Sophie Rodrique for her PR infusion of energy and guidance just when I needed it. To my amazing supporters, dog walking pack, and idea generators, Sandy, Ali, and Pam.

To my sister, Pollie, thank you for your role modeling in life, for being my first reader, and for always encouraging me as we both look for our paths together and separately.

To my family, Caroline, Sam, and Dusty, for their tolerance as I navigate unchartered territory and patience as I learn to improve.

My grandmother, who taught me grammar, and my incredible mother-in-law never stopped writing; thank you for your commitment to your own writing. I stand on your shoulders with this work. And to my mom for all of your support and for teaching me the power of a thank-you note—thank you all.

Endnotes

1   Cuddy, Amy. "Your Body Language May Shape Who You Are." TED Talk, June 2012. https://www.ted.com/talks/amy_cuddy_your_body_language_may_shape_who_you_are?utm_campaign=tedspread&utm_medium=referral&utm_source=tedcomshare.

2   Buckingham, Marcus. *Love and work how to find what you love, Love what you do, and do it for the rest of your life Marcus Buckingham.* Boston: Harvard Business Review Press, April 5, 2022.

3   Oppland, Mike. "8 Traits of Flow According to Mihaly Csikszentmihalyi." Positive Psychology, December 16, 2016. Accessed July 22, 2024. https://positivepsychology.com/mihaly-csikszentmihalyi-father-of-flow/.

4   Psychology Today Staff. "Myers-Briggs." Psychology Today. Accessed July 22, 2024. https://www.psychologytoday.com/us/basics/myers-briggs#:~:text=The%20MBTI%20was%20initially%20developed,created%20by%20psychoanalyst%20Carl%20Jung.6.

5   Jeffrey, Joyann. "Study Finds Which US States Have the Fastest and Slowest Talkers." TODAY.com, January 25, 2023. https://www.today.com/news/study-finds-us-states-fastest-slowest-talkers-rcna67388.

6   "William Moulton Marston." INTERNATIONAL DISC INSTITUTE, November 26, 2023. https://interdisc.org/william-moulton-marston/.

7   Mcleod, Saul. "Maslow's Hierarchy of Needs." Simply Psychology, January 24, 2024. https://www.simplypsychology.org/maslow.html.

8   Hobsbawm, Julia, *The Nowhere Office: Reinventing Work and the Workplace of the Future.* New York: Hachette Book Group. April 12, 2022.

9   https://www.goodreads.com/author/quotes/8435.Norman_Vincent_Peale

10 Collins, Jim. *Good to Great: Why Some Companies Make the Leap… and Others Don't.* New York: HarperCollins Publishers, Inc. 2001.

11 Frankl, Viktor E. *Man's Search for Meaning: An Introduction to Logotherapy.* Boston: Beacon Press, October 23, 1984.

12 Murphy, Mark. "Neuroscience Explains Why You Need to Write down Your Goals If You Actually Want to Achieve Them." Forbes, February 20, 2024. https://www.forbes.com/sites/markmurphy/2018/04/15/neuroscience-explains-why-you-need-to-write-down-your-goals-if-you-actually-want-to-achieve-them/.

13 Wu, Jade. "5 Ways to Use Positive Self-Talk to Psych Yourself Up." Edited by Matt Huston. Psychology Today. Accessed July 22, 2024. https://www.psychologytoday.com/us/blog/the-savvy-psychologist/202103/5-ways-to-use-positive-self-talk-to-psych-yourself-up.

14 Napolean Hill https://www.goodreads.com/author/quotes/399.Napoleon_Hill

15 Nevins, Mark. "What Are Your Big Rocks?" Forbes, February 20, 2024. https://www.forbes.com/sites/hillennevins/2020/01/21/what-are-your-big-rocks/.

16 Covey, Stephen. 1989. *The 7 Habits of Highly Effective People.* New York: Free Press.

17 Waytz, Adam. "Beware- A Culture of Busyness: Organizations Must Stop Conflating Activity with Achievement." Harvard Business Review, March-April 2023.

18 Zak, Heidi. "Adults Make More than 35,000 Decisions per Day. Here Are 4 Ways to Prevent Mental Burnout ." Inc., January 21, 2020. https://www.inc.com/heidi-zak/adults-make-more-than-35000-decisions-per-day-here-are-4-ways-to-prevent-mental-burnout.html.

19   Gross, Terry. "Stephen King: 'My Imagination Was Very Active - Even at a Young Age.'" NPR, July 27, 2018. https://www.npr.org/2018/07/27/633002291/stephen-king-my-imagination-was-very-active-even-at-a-young-age.

20   Haden, Jeff. "Neuroscience Says Your Brain Is Wired to Procrastinate: 4 Simple Ways to Stop Putting off Important Things (No Willpower Required) ." Inc., September 9, 2019. https://www.inc.com/jeff-haden/neuroscience-says-your-brain-is-wired-to-procrastinate-4-simple-ways-to-stop-putting-off-important-things-willpower-not-required.html.

21   Hari, Johann. *Stolen Focus: Why You Can't Pay Attention and How to Think Deeply Again* Crown, 2021.

22   DePaul, Kristi. "What Does It Really Take to Build a New Habit?" Harvard Business Review, February 2, 2021. https://hbr.org/2021/02/what-does-it-really-take-to-build-a-new-habit.

23   Clear, James, *Atomic Habits: Tiny Changes, Remarkable Results: An Easy & Proven Way to Build Good Habits & Break Bad Ones.* New York, New York, Avery, an imprint of Penguin Random House, 2018.

24   Hari, Johann. *Stolen Focus: Why You Can't Pay Attention and How to Think Deeply Again* Crown, 2021.

25   Hari, Johann. *Stolen Focus: Why You Can't Pay Attention and How to Think Deeply Again* Crown, 2021.

26   Thorne, Blake. "How Distractions at Work Take up More Time than You Think." I DONE This, October 21, 2023. https://blog.idonethis.com/distractions-at-work/.

27   Thorne, Blake. "How Distractions at Work Take up More Time than You Think." I DONE This, October 21, 2023. https://blog.idonethis.com/distractions-at-work/.

28   Grant, Adam, 1981-, *Think Again: The Power of Knowing What You Don't Know.* [New York, New York], Viking, an imprint of Penguin Random House LLC, 2021.

29   Jenniges, Sam, *Recognition Rebooted.* [United States], Sandra K Jenniges, 2019.

30   Goldman, Daniel. *Emotional Intelligence, Why it Can Matter More than IQ.* 1995

31   Bradberry, Travis, and Jean Greaves. *Emotional Intelligence 2.0.* San Diego, CA: TalentSmart. 2009.

32   Huffington, Arianna. *The Sleep Revolution: Transforming Your Life, One Night at a Time.* New York: Harmony Books, 2016.

33   Huffington, Arianna. *The Sleep Revolution: Transforming Your Life, One Night at a Time.* New York: Harmony Books, 2016.

34   Huffington, Arianna. The Sleep Revolution: Transforming Your Life, One Night at a Time. New York: Harmony Books, 2016.

35   Pollan, Michael. *The Omnivore's Dilemma.* London, England: Bloomsbury Publishing PLC. 2011.

36   "Physical Activity Guidelines for Americans ." health.gov. Accessed July 23, 2024. https://health.gov/our-work/nutrition-physical-activity/physical-activity-guidelines/current-guidelines.

37   "Physical Activity Guidelines for Americans." health.gov. Accessed July 23, 2024. https://health.gov/our-work/nutrition-physical-activity/physical-activity-guidelines/current-guidelines.

38   Oxford English Dictionary, 2016: online.

39   Wolpe, Rabbi David. "We Are Defining Love the Wrong Way." Time, February 16, 2016. https://time.com/4225777/meaning-of-love/.

40   "Emotional Wellness Toolkit." National Institutes of Health, August 8, 2022. https://www.nih.gov/health-information/emotional-wellness-toolkit.

41   Mayo Clinic Staff. "Chronic Stress Puts Your Health at Risk." Mayo Clinic, August 1, 2023. https://www.mayoclinic.org/healthy-lifestyle/stress-management/in-depth/stress/art-20046037.

42   "How Five-Finger Breathing Can Bring on Deep Relaxation." Cleveland Clinic, January 27, 2023. https://health.clevelandclinic.org/five-finger-breathing.

43   Berman, M. G., Stier, A. J., & Akcelik, G. N. (2019). Environmental neuroscience. American Psychologist, 74(9), 1039–1052. https://doi.org/10.1037/amp0000583.

44   Thoreau, Henry David. *Walden*. Black and White Classics, 2014.

45   Maté, Gabor, and Daniel Maté. *The myth of normal: Trauma, illness, and healing in a toxic culture*. New York: Penguin Audio, 2022.

46   Ross, Ashley. "How Meditation Went Mainstream." Time, March 9, 2016. https://time.com/4246928/meditation-history-buddhism/.

47   Meraji, Shereen Marisol, and Sylvie Douglis. "Mindfulness 101: How to Begin a Meditation Practice." NPR, January 3, 2022. https://www.npr.org/2021/12/21/1066585316/mindfulness-meditation-with-john-kabat-zinn.

48   Meraji, Shereen Marisol, and Sylvie Douglis. "Mindfulness 101: How to Begin a Meditation Practice." NPR, January 3, 2022. https://www.npr.org/2021/12/21/1066585316/mindfulness-meditation-with-john-kabat-zinn.

49   Tolle, Eckhart, 1948-, *A New Earth: Awakening to Your Life's Purpose*. New York, N.Y., Dutton/Penguin Group, 2005.

50   Šimić, Goran, Mladenka Tkalčić, Vana Vukić, Damir Mulc, Ena Španić, Marina Šagud, Francisco E Olucha-Bordonau, Mario Vukšić, and Patrick R Hof. "Understanding Emotions: Origins and Roles of the Amygdala." Biomolecules, May 31, 2021. https://www.ncbi.nlm.nih.gov/pmc/articles/PMC8228195/.

51   Achor, Shawn. *The Happiness Advantage: The Seven Principles that Fuel Success and Performance at Work*. New York: Crown Publishing Group, 2010.

52   Sutton, Jeremy. "Is Happiness Genetic? An Update on Recent Research." PositivePsychology.com, July 21, 2019. https://positivepsychology.com/is-happiness-genetic/.

53   Newton, Claire. "Circles of Control." Claire Newton. Accessed July 23, 2024. https://www.clairenewton.co.za/my-articles/circles-of-control.html.

54   Newton, Claire. "Circles of Control." Claire Newton. Accessed July 23, 2024. https://www.clairenewton.co.za/my-articles/circles-of-control.html.

About the Author

Mazie Minehart Colen has dedicated over thirty years to working with executive clients, helping individuals and organizations achieve higher performance. Her career began with consulting for Microsoft and Merck, where she developed her coaching methodology. Since then, Mazie has become a sought-after catalyst for transformative change, influencing leaders across diverse sectors—from innovative startups to Fortune 500 giants. Her reputation, built solely through referrals, reflects her exceptional ability to guide individuals at every leadership level toward extraordinary success.

Beyond her professional achievements, Mazie treasures quality time with her husband, two children, and their labradoodle, Stella. She embraces an active lifestyle, delighting in family surf days, boating, hiking, and savoring every moment by the ocean.

? pts of power?

Made in United States
North Haven, CT
04 September 2024

56934630R00085